Freely Gathered Communities of Faith and the Changes between the Testaments

Freely Gathered Communities of Faith and the Changes between the Testaments

M. A. ERICKSON

foreword by Roger D. Cotton

WIPF & STOCK · Eugene, Oregon

FREELY GATHERED COMMUNITIES OF FAITH AND
THE CHANGES BETWEEN THE TESTAMENTS

Copyright © 2019 M. A. Erickson. All rights reserved. Except for brief quotations in critical publications or reviews, no part of this book may be reproduced in any manner without prior written permission from the publisher. Write: Permissions, Wipf and Stock Publishers, 199 W. 8th Ave., Suite 3, Eugene, OR 97401.

Unless otherwise noted, Scripture quotations are from The Holy Bible, English Standard Version ® (ESV®), copyright 2001 by Crossway, a publishing ministry of Good News Publishers. Used by permission. All rights reserved.

Scripture quotations labeled NASB are from the New American Standard Bible ®, copyright 1960, 1962, 1963, 1968, 1971, 1972, 1973, 1975, 1977, 1995 by The Lockman Foundation. Used by permission.

Wipf & Stock
An Imprint of Wipf and Stock Publishers
199 W. 8th Ave., Suite 3
Eugene, OR 97401

www.wipfandstock.com

PAPERBACK ISBN: 978-1-5326-9250-5
HARDCOVER ISBN: 978-1-5326-9251-2
EBOOK ISBN: 978-1-5326-9252-9

Manufactured in the U.S.A. 04/18/19

Contents

Foreword by Roger D. Cotton		vii
Acknowledgements		ix
List of Abbreviations		xi
1	How Do We Understand the Tremendous Changes between the Testaments?	1
2	Searching For Answers	8
3	A Methodology for Analyzing Change	28
4	Changes Regarding the Land	32
5	Changes Regarding the Use of the Sword	55
6	Changes Regarding the Temple	77
7	Contrasts between the Old Testament Nation and the New Testament Communities of Faith in Christ	103
8	The Paradigm Shift and its Implications for Today	114
Bibliography		123

Foreword

BY DR. ROGER COTTON
PROFESSOR OF OLD TESTAMENT, ASSEMBLIES OF GOD
THEOLOGICAL SEMINARY (SPRINGFIELD, MO)

Mark Erickson has written on a subject of great usefulness to all who want to relate the Old Testament to the New—three key subjects in the discontinuity and continuity between the two Testaments. He explains the discontinuity between the two through the land, the sword and the temple. The choice of these three subjects gets at the heart of some of the most important questions about the Bible. Many people struggle with the warfare or use of the sword in the Old Testament. The land is conspicuously absent in the New Testament and the temple worship system of the Old Testament still seems to many Bible readers to be somehow important today. However, a closer look at the New Testament shows that the writers reinterpret these three for God's people under the New Covenant. Erickson's understanding of these three very effectively opens up key principles of the continuity and discontinuity between the testaments. His key understanding is the same as what I have come to, which is that Israel was a nation raised up by God in the ancient Near East to prepare for Christ and Christians now only form freely gathered communities of faith in the work of God's Kingdom. Therefore, Christians do not have a land, use the sword in their own armed forces, and do not have a specific temple worship system to adhere to because, with the coming of Christ, God's people are

FOREWORD

no longer a geo-political nation in the world and this is what the temple system was preparing the world for.

This book was originally Erickson's dissertation and is very well focused, researched, and organized. He has done solid exegesis and this is an excellent representation of biblical theology, which is the study of the message of the Bible writers in their own terms, in the context of their own issues, and then ultimately in the context of the message of the whole of the Scriptures. His conclusions make the best sense of the continuity and discontinuity of the testaments. Erickson is very level-headed and orthodox in his theology. This book makes a very relevant and solid contribution to biblical theology and the understanding of the Old Testament in relation to the New Testament and in relation to Christians today.

Acknowledgements

The book that follows is based on the dissertation I completed in May of 2018, which led to my graduation from Global University in June of 2018 with a Doctor of Ministry degree. A few stylistic and wording changes have been made, to facilitate readability in a book format. In the process I included some additional paragraphs in regard to land and temple, to bring things into better focus for current readers.

There are many people who made this project possible:

My wife, Marian, made many sacrifices so that I could complete the dissertation on which this book is based, and I simply could not have done it without her. Her patience and support have been amazing. She also encouraged and even exhorted me in the final leg of the journey, to complete the task at hand and finish the project. My son Luke also gave encouragement and support at many points along the way—a refreshing balm to the heart of a father. My mother, Carol Erickson, (and late father John Erickson), provided the initial impetus and ongoing support for my ministry and academic pursuits. The support of family and friends has been indispensable.

Dr. Jim Richardson was my advisor and mentor, and as the Director of Doctoral Studies assisted me in numerous ways. His encouragement and guidance came through at many crucial points, for which I am deeply grateful. Dr. Roger Cotton gave guidance and insight regarding the Old Testament and biblical theology, which were crucial for this study. His mentoring and advice had a major impact. Dr. Carl Chrisner provided support and guidance

Acknowledgements

as a mentor and leader, and the course that he authored had a deep personal impact on me. Dr. Randy Hedlun gave key encouragement that helped me complete the journey, and was instrumental, along with Steve Handy, in helping me to sharpen my awareness of current theological issues. My additional graduate course mentors, Dr. Clinton Caszatt, Dr. Robert Caldwell, and Dr. Robert Stanford, each brought the impact of their expertise to bear on my academic studies in vital ways, for which I am very grateful.

I also wish to thank the Alliance for Assemblies of God Higher Education for the generous scholarship which helped me complete my doctoral studies; I am also deeply appreciative of the support of Global University. This word of thanks must go out to the entire leadership team at Global University for making assistance possible for those seeking to further their education. Special thanks are also due to the proficient and dedicated Global University staff members who assisted me in numerous capacities along the way—particularly the Student Services staff and those in the Graduate School of Theology. I also thank Heather Van Allen for her assistance with proofreading, editing, and grammatical suggestions.

Above all, I must give glory to God alone for his grace and sufficiency. The glory of God as reflected in His Son reaches far beyond all human attempts to make it known.

List of Abbreviations

ANE	Ancient Near East
AJPS	Asian Journal of Pentecostal Studies
BSac	Bibliotheca Sacra
cf.	confer (Latin). Compare.
DNTB	Dictionary of New Testament Background: A Compendium of Contemporary Biblical Scholarship
DOTP	Dictionary of the Old Testament: Pentateuch
EDT	Evangelical Dictionary of Theology
ESV	English Standard Version (2001)
JETS	Journal of the Evangelical Theological Society
JQJLT	Judaism: A Quarterly Journal of Jewish Life and Thought
JSNT	Journal for the Study of the New Testament
JSOT	Journal for the Study of the Old Testament
JTSA	Journal of Theology for Southern Africa
NASB	New American Standard Bible (1995)
NT	New Testament
OT	Old Testament
SBL	Society of Biblical Literature
SVTQ	St. Vladimir's Theological Quarterly

1

How Do We Understand the Tremendous Changes between the Testaments?

INTRODUCTION

The changes between the Old and New Testament are massive, when one considers the full range of issues involved. Food laws, civil laws with their penalties, animal sacrifices and the temple priesthood, circumcision, and other OT regulations are set aside as requirements for the NT communities of faith. The land, the sword, and the temple are reinterpreted in the NT. Jesus fulfills the law, and the NT incorporates both Jews and Gentiles who believe in the Messiah Jesus as members of the household of God.

Rather than attempting to address all of these changes individually, a narrower scope will be in view here. Three major areas of change will be explored in light of the biblical texts and contemporary scholarship: land, sword, and temple. Then, the changes between the OT and NT in these three areas are examined in light of the difference between God's instructions for a nation (Israel) in the OT, and God's instructions for freely gathered communities of faith in Christ in the NT. The OT nation had divine land promises, while the NT communities existed in various cities and towns in the Roman Empire without divine promises to obtain land. The OT nation of Israel had use of the sword and engaged in battle with other nations, while a dramatic shift is obvious with regard to the NT communities of faith. The focus on the OT temple is also transformed in the NT and the NT communities become the temple of God. What are the central reasons for these changes, and why did they occur?

STATEMENT OF THE PROBLEM

The issue of continuity and discontinuity between the Old and New Testament has been discussed and debated since the time of the early church. The major differences between the OT and NT presented many questions in need of explanation. Because of major differences between the OT and NT, Marcion's solution was to claim there were different gods for each testament. The church rejected this solution, and as the church expanded into the Greek-speaking world, allegorical interpretations of the OT were often used by various church fathers to make the OT more palatable to ancient Greco-Roman societies.[1] The influence of Origen and Augustine guaranteed that allegory would continue to be influential into the Middle Ages and beyond.[2] Today, the allegorical method has been largely set aside because of its lack of correspondence with the intended meaning of the original human author.

The Reformation brought a renewed interest in the historical context of Scripture and the consideration of authorial intent,[3] although allegorical interpretation was still utilized in some areas. The various strands of thought in the faith communities unleashed by the Reformation led over time to multiple approaches to the question of continuity and discontinuity between the OT and NT.

Since the Reformation, areas of continuity and discontinuity have been addressed by Reformed-Covenant theology,

---

1. Petersen, "Debate throughout Church History," 299–330.
2. Petersen, "Debate throughout Church History," 351–81.
3. Petersen, "Debate throughout Church History," 430–32.

Lutheranism, Dispensational theology, historical-critical methods, Theonomy, Zionism, and other theological approaches. While there are significant areas of common ground in the quest to explain discontinuities, thorny problems and differences of interpretation remain. The issue of discontinuity has tended to become a captive of the theological system which is addressing the problem, resulting in widely divergent answers in some areas. Theological systems of interpretation have provided varying solutions to explain both the continuity and discontinuity between the OT and NT.[4]

To narrow the focus, the primary research here involves three specific areas of discontinuity between the OT nation (Israel) and the freely gathered communities of faith in the NT. The land, the sword, and the temple are analyzed to show how these three areas undergo major transformation in the NT.

The Rationale for this Study and the Purpose of the Research

The rationale for this study has been to determine, by examining the above areas of change between the OT and the NT in light of the thesis and in light of contemporary scholarship, whether or not the change to "freely gathered communities of faith in Christ" would be the solution to explain many of the changes between the OT and NT. The purpose of the research has been to examine key areas of discontinuity between the OT and NT in order to gain a clear understanding of what those changes were, and why they occurred. By investigating the three major areas noted above in light of their biblical context and the contributions of contemporary scholarship, the issue of discontinuity in these areas is brought into focus. Then, these discontinuities are examined in relation to the thesis of this study, to see if it provides a sound rationale for explaining the discontinuities. Chapter 4 explores how the focus on land is transformed when moving from the OT to the NT; Chapter 5 investigates the use of the sword in the OT and how that changes in the

---

4. Feinberg, "Systems of Discontinuity," 1233-417.

NT; and Chapter 6 examines the way in which the emphasis on the temple undergoes change.

A secondary purpose of this study is to examine whether the solution that has been proposed may also provide an approach that will be effective to explain differences between the OT and NT to people in contemporary cultures. This will be addressed in the concluding section of the study. Since differences between the OT and NT remain an area of confusion and misunderstanding in contemporary life, any progress that is made through this or other studies may provide needed clarity in this area. It is possible that the thesis may be used to explain additional discontinuities between the OT and NT beyond the scope of this study.

A Proposed Solution: The Thesis of the Study

The central thesis is that many areas of discontinuity between the OT and the NT can best be explained as differences between God's instructions for a specific nation (Israel) in the OT, and God's instructions for the freely gathered communities of faith in Christ in the NT. This proposed solution is the result of years of study. By identifying the NT body of Christ as "freely gathered communities of faith in Christ," a number of significant areas will be addressed and a unique contribution can be made by providing additional clarity regarding various changes that took place. Freely gathered communities that are based on faith in Christ in the NT can be shown to correspond with changes regarding OT land promises, the use of the sword, the meaning of the OT temple, and other issues.

"Freely gathered" means that the NT communities are not ethnically or nationally comprised. They are made up of individuals who have responded to the gospel by faith in Christ and have joined together on that basis. "Communities" highlights the contrast with "nation" as well as the fact that there are specific boundaries to these communities which are very different than the national boundaries of OT Israel. The NT communities exist in many cities and towns among the nations, on a different basis than Jewish communities or the Jewish nation.

"Faith in Christ" as highlighted in the thesis is central to the NT communities and, among other things, is used to identify the enlarged people of God that is made up of both Jews and Gentiles.[5] Faith in Christ is foundational to the new communities. Christ is central to the OT and the NT, and Christ fulfills many OT promises. Christ as Messiah is the foundation for the new communities of faith, and the new communities exist among the nations with different boundaries in many respects than OT Israel.

Definition of Terms

The term *discontinuity* as it is used in this study is not referring to "contradictions" between the OT and NT, but refers rather to major changes between the Testaments. *Discontinuity* is the theological term that is commonly used to identify these changes. *Continuity* as it is used in this study refers to areas where presuppositions, doctrines, and other teachings continue from the OT to the NT. *Canonical* is a term that refers to the canon of Scripture, and is identified as sixty-six books: the thirty-nine books of the OT and the twenty-seven books of the NT.[6] Debates about the Apocrypha will not be considered, since the Apocrypha is considered here to be outside of the canonical OT and NT Scriptures. *Intertextuality* is a methodological term for this study and because the definition involves more lengthy explanation and analysis, this term will be defined in the chapter on methodology. The term *sword* will be used throughout the study as a symbol for the use of lethal force in the OT and NT, while recognizing that other methods were also used to inflict death.

Boundaries for the Study

The sixty-six canonical books of the OT and NT are the main boundaries for the study and provide a definite set of texts as translated by the ESV in this study. The OT canonical books are seen to

---

5. Burge, *Jesus and the Land*, 1784–90; 1526–33.
6. Blomberg et al., *Introduction to Biblical Interpretation*, 150.

represent, as reliably as is currently possible based on modern textual criticism, the OT Scriptures;[7] these OT writings are acknowledged here as the books that were accepted as God's Word by the Jewish people of the first century AD.[8]

The meaning of the OT texts are to be determined within their original literary context, and then related to NT interpretation and fulfillment. The canonical texts of the OT provided God's instruction for the OT nation, and the canonical texts of the NT provide God's instruction for the NT communities that are based on faith in Christ. This approach recognizes that the teaching of Christ and the apostles provided God's instruction in oral form to NT followers of Christ before becoming consolidated into the canonical NT texts. It also recognizes that there are various processes by which the OT canon came to be developed and accepted. But there will be no attempt to go "behind" the texts into the complex debates about oral and written sources and other factors.

Another limitation is that the study primarily focuses on discontinuities between the OT and NT that are related to the three themes of land, sword, and temple. These three themes are then related to the thesis to see if the thesis provides a sound explanation for the changes that took place in these three areas. Contemporary scholarship has been examined for insights regarding the three themes. So the interplay in this study is between the themes of land, sword, and temple in the canonical texts of the Old and New Testaments along with insights of current scholarship regarding those themes and the thesis as an explanation for the discontinuities. New solutions are being sought to shed light on the issue of discontinuity.

Basic Assumptions

The divine inspiration of the OT and NT writings is a basic assumption for this study. The discontinuities between the OT and the NT are not a "problem" if one takes the position that the OT and NT books involved are simply diverse religious writings that

7. Blomberg et al., *Introduction to Biblical Interpretation*, 150.
8. Blomberg et al., *Introduction to Biblical Interpretation*, 104–9.

were collected over time into an OT collection and a NT collection. But a basic presupposition for many forms of Christian theology throughout the centuries which is also followed in this study is that the OT and NT writings were inspired by the one Holy Spirit, even though there were diverse human authors, circumstances, and time periods for these writings. The underlying concept of divine inspiration means that many reasons for discontinuity can be sought and found.[9] This is supported by the widely accepted observation that many texts in the NT are directly explaining areas of OT fulfillment and supply reasons for the changes brought about since the coming of Jesus as the Messiah.

In addition to divine inspiration, an underlying presupposition accepted here is that the Bible must first of all interpret itself and more specifically, that the NT must be authoritative in interpreting the OT. Bruce Waltke notes that "the classical rule *sacra scriptura sui ipsius interpres* (the Bible interprets itself)—more specifically, the New interprets the Old—should be accepted by all Christian theologians."[10] There is no attempt here to develop a "new hermeneutic" that flies in the face of the NT interpretation of the OT. While some contemporary scholars disagree with the way NT authors interpret OT texts and claim a higher methodology (from a 20th or 21st century perspective) than that of Jesus and the apostles,[11] this has led to pitting the OT against the NT and other errors. R. W. Wall notes that "the current reductionism of interpreting the OT or NT in isolation from the other, thereby regarding the NT's relationship to the Hebrew Bible as insignificant, is subverted by the NT's appeal to and exegesis of the OT."[12] Divine inspiration is a presupposition for this study which provides a key underpinning for the NT use of the OT and the relationships between the Testaments. The OT texts should be studied in their original context first, and then related to NT usage and interpretation.

9. While there are various levels at which a rational basis for the presupposition of divine inspiration can be investigated, it is here assumed rather than being discussed at length.

10. Waltke, "Kingdom Promises," 5451–53.

11. Beale, *Handbook*, 100.

12. Wall, "Intertextuality, Biblical," 546.

2

Searching For Answers

SEARCHING FOR AN EFFECTIVE explanation for discontinuities between the OT and NT is rather like untying the Gordian Knot. One must analyze a sufficient number of discontinuities to demonstrate the explanatory power of a cohesive thesis to address the problem in a significant way. But this involves tracing various major themes in order to investigate how they are transformed when moving from the OT to the NT and then analyzing whether or not the thesis provides an effective explanation. The themes chosen here (land, sword, and temple) provide a minimal number of themes to demonstrate the effectiveness of the thesis presented here. But if one were to review the literature that simply touches on any of these areas, the number of works in current academia and church history that do so would number in the thousands, if not the tens of thousands.

So is there no way to investigate such meta-themes to try to shed new light on what has been a very perplexing problem? The approach here is to limit such review primarily to authors who examine not only the above stated themes, but who focus on the *transformation* of these themes when moving from OT to NT. In addition, the many rabbit trails that could be sparked by this discussion will be walled off, and substantive footnotes will be used at times to touch on specific issues that need to be briefly mentioned.

Notable contributions will be mentioned but primarily as they relate to the thesis—since what is being sought after is new solutions to a problem that has defied a simple solution (some would add that this issue has *never* been solved to a satisfactory degree). This study is not an attempt to provide a one size fits all solution to the complex issue of discontinuity between the OT and NT but attempts to shed light on a key comparative issue between the canonical OT and NT texts in regard to discontinuity.

Comparison between God's instructions in the OT for the nation of Israel and God's instructions for freely gathered communities of faith in Christ in the NT *as a primary interpretive explanation for discontinuities* between the OT and NT has not been stated as such in current literature. The comparative link between the OT nation and NT body of Christ has been pointed out in relation to discontinuity, however. As Roger Cotton notes, "the major discontinuity is in the use of a nation, Israel, which God established in the OT, to prepare for Christ. Now, in the NT, the people of God are not a nation in a certain land but are the spiritual body of Christ living among the nations."[1] This study develops a more specific focus on the NT communities, defined as freely gathered communities based on faith in Jesus Christ that are composed of both Jews and Gentiles. This specific focus provides a number of contrasts with the OT nation.

Ellen Christiansen focused on boundary differences between the OT nation of Israel and the NT communities, and included significant comparisons based on corporate identity, boundary markers, holiness, belonging, and how relationship with God was defined.[2] However, the major point of comparison in that study was on water baptism as the replacement for circumcision as a boundary and identity marker,[3] rather than on the contrast between the OT nation and NT communities of faith in Christ as a key for explaining a large number of discontinuities between the OT and NT.

---

1. Cotton, "Old Testament Theology," 83.
2. Christiansen, *Ritual Boundaries*.
3. Christiansen, *Ritual Boundaries*, 302–7.

In *Integrative Theology*, Bruce Demarest and Gordon Lewis develop a scheme of interpretation described as "spiritual–institutional theology."[4] In this scheme, "major similarities exist between Israel and the church spiritually and major dissimilarities exist structurally or institutionally."[5] Spiritual differences between the old and new covenants are also acknowledged.[6] The church is said to be a very different institution.[7] Various differences between the institutions of the church and the nation of Israel are highlighted, and this explains some of the significant discontinuities between the OT and NT.[8] However, the thesis developed here goes further by contrasting God's instructions to a nation in the OT with God's instructions to freely gathered communities of faith in Christ as the explanation for many discontinuities. Spiritual–institutional theology also has a broader theological focus by relating to four distinct theologies in an attempt to integrate "the covenants, promises, kingdom, and dispensations of the four major single-theme theologies."[9] The focus of this study is not to develop a complete theological system but to provide a clearer explanation of discontinuities between the OT and NT, while accepting the presupposition of the divine inspiration of both the OT and NT.

In *Continuity and Discontinuity: Perspectives on the Relationship between the Old and New Testaments*, essays are presented by various scholars to examine issues of continuity and discontinuity between the OT and NT.[10] Themes of salvation, law, the people of God, and kingdom promises are examined in relation to continuity and discontinuity between the OT and NT. However, the issue of continuity and discontinuity is primarily addressed within the theological system of the presenters, whether from a Dispensationalist,

---

4. Demarest and Lewis, *Integrative Theology* (vol. 3), 340–42.
5. Demarest and Lewis, *Integrative Theology* (vol. 3), 340.
6. Demarest and Lewis, *Integrative Theology* (vol. 3), 341.
7. Demarest and Lewis, *Integrative Theology* (vol. 3), 339.
8. Demarest and Lewis, *Integrative Theology* (vol. 3), 339–41.
9. Demarest and Lewis, *Integrative Theology* (vol. 3), 342.
10. Feinberg, *Continuity and Discontinuity*.

Reformed-covenant, or Promise-fulfillment perspective.[11] Explaining discontinuities within these systems has led to divergent viewpoints that have at times been difficult to reconcile. This study will not develop a complete theological system of interpretation but will focus instead on utilizing the thesis to explain discontinuities. This will hopefully provide a different vantage point to provide explanations for a number of discontinuities in a clear fashion. In reviewing the literature, in addition to the focus of the thesis, the subtopics of land, sword, and temple have been examined.

LITERATURE REVIEW ON THE LAND

The theme of land when moving from OT to NT has not been a major theological focus until recent times.[12] In reviewing contemporary literature on the theme of land, W. D. Davies contributed a major study on the land in the OT and NT entitled *The Gospel and the Land: Early Christianity and Jewish Territorial Doctrine* (1974). Gerhard von Rad had penned a brief article on the land some time earlier[13] which both Davies (1974) and Walter Brueggemann (1977)[14] cite in their works. Davies went on to trace the concept of the land through the OT, the intertestamental period, and the NT, noting changes that occurred. Numerous scholars have utilized the work of Davies and developed (or in some cases challenged) his observations and interpretations. Contemporary studies have often further developed or refined the conclusions of Davies that the land promises are transformed in the NT to a focus on the person of Christ.[15] Oren Martin points out that Davies "spiritualizes the land and relocates it to Christ."[16] He claims that "this view does not

11. Feinberg, *Continuity and Discontinuity*, 22–78.
12. Martens, "Reading the Earth Story," 226; Martin, *Promised Land*, 18–19.
13. von Rad, "Yahweh's Land in the Hexateuch."
14. Brueggemann, *The Land: Place as Gift*.
15. See Martin, *Promised Land*, 118–51, 159; Wright, *Paul and the Faithfulness of God*, 11007–29; Burge, *Jesus and the Land*, 1085–44; 1775–87; Davies, *Gospel and the Land*, 179; 367–70; Robertson, "New Covenant Perspective," 135–40; Walker, "Land in the Apostles Writings," 84–88.
16. Martin, *Promised Land*, 19.

sufficiently present the New Testament fulfillment of what the Old Testament anticipated"[17] and offers further refinements.

In *The Land: Place as Gift, Promise, and Challenge to Biblical Faith*, Walter Brueggemann's approach contrasts in some ways with that of Davies. Brueggemann focuses on a more earthly conception of land in the NT. Jesus returns the dispossessed to their land in the NT,[18] but those who grasp the land will lose it.[19] Land is given a dialectic twist here, but the emphasis on land in this age in the NT seems overstated. Brueggemann claims that "land is a central, if not *the central theme* of biblical faith" (italics his).[20] This, too, seems overstated even though land is a significant feature of biblical theology. Other contemporary issues regarding the land are also debated in current scholarly circles which are beyond the scope of this study.[21]

O. Palmer Robertson examines the relationship between OT and NT perspectives on the land in terms of the new covenant. The land promises are traced between the canonical texts as OT prophetic shadows and types that become NT realities.[22] The land promises of the OT are fulfilled "in terms of the newly re-created cosmos about which the apostle Paul speaks in Romans."[23] In the

---

17. Martin, *Promised Land*, 19.

18. Brueggemann, *The Land: Place as Gift*, 163.

19. Brueggemann, *The Land: Place as Gift*, 164.

20. Brueggemann, *The Land: Place as Gift*, 3.

21. The issue of the land promises to OT Israel impacts contemporary scholarship in some debated areas. How valid are the OT land promises for Israel today, and is Israel currently fulfilling these OT land promises? Theological positions range from weak or minimal support for the application of OT land promises to Israel today, to strong support of such OT fulfillments (Gregerman, "Hermeneutical Approaches to the Land," 413–20). A related issue is the applicability of OT land promises to a literal fulfillment in a thousand year millennial reign of Christ over the land of Israel (Townsend, "Fulfillment of the Land Promise," 320–34). Some see the OT land promises for Israel only being fulfilled in the millennial reign of Christ (Witmer, "Romans," 453–54). While these are significant issues, they have to do with intermediate prophetic fulfillments that are beyond the NT period and prior to the new heavens and the new earth and, as such, are beyond the scope and purpose of the present study.

22. Robertson, "New Covenant Perspective," 125–26; 135–36.

23. Robertson, "New Covenant Perspective," 136.

SEARCHING FOR ANSWERS

new covenant fulfillment of the land theme from the OT, "the land has expanded to encompass the cosmos."[24] Similarly, in *The Land in the Apostles' Writings*, Peter Walker examines the writings of Paul and posits that the OT land was a great metaphor for the ultimate purpose of God to "eventually bring the whole world into submission to his healing reign."[25]

In *Jesus and the Land* (2010), Gary Burge developed a significant study on the land theme. Here, the issue of land is examined first of all from an OT perspective and then how the land theme was transformed by Jesus and the apostles. Significant points from the Gospels, Acts, Paul's writings, and other NT documents are developed to show that the OT land is transformed to a focus on Christ in the NT[26] as well as the eventual heavenly renewal of the earth.[27] One point of debate is how Burge traces the theme of land into recent history and current events, a point which will not be attempted in this study.

Oren Martin (2015) developed a major study of the land theme in relation to God's overall redemptive plan. The land is traced, beginning in Eden, through the OT, and to the ultimate fulfillment in the new heavens and new earth.[28] The themes of temple and Jerusalem are also tied to the land by Martin,[29] as well as various other scholars. T. Desmond Alexander (2008) traces the theme of God's dwelling place from Eden to the OT tabernacle/temple, the NT church, and ultimately the New Jerusalem.[30] The land figures significantly in Alexander's survey since the OT dwelling place is linked to the land, and the land theme is transformed in the NT.

In *God's People in God's Land* (1990), Christopher Wright focuses on the OT nation, tribe, and family unit in relation to God and the land. Property rights, inheritance laws, and other aspects of life

---

24. Robertson, "New Covenant Perspective," 139.
25. Walker, "Land in the Apostles Writings," 87.
26. Burge, *Jesus and the Land*, 1112–20.
27. Burge, *Jesus and the Land*, 1842–47.
28. Martin, *Promised Land*, 31–116; 117–57.
29. Martin, *Promised Land*, 155–57.
30. Alexander, *Eden to the New Jerusalem*.

on the land are carefully examined. Moving forward, he identifies a transformation where "Christ himself takes over the significance and function of the land kinship qualification,"[31] and parallels are drawn between Christ and the land. This is identified as a typological fulfillment.[32] Again, transformation is identified when moving from the OT land vision to the NT.

Karen Wenell (2007) investigates the concept of land and temple as sacred spaces from OT to NT along with an analysis of the relationship of Jesus to the land. She concludes, in part, that the message of Jesus "establishes a new sacred space, and a new relationship with God, people, and kingdom."[33] Its boundaries were open to provide a place for those on the outside "and for those without status or position."[34] Regarding the land, Jesus' message of the kingdom "evokes the promises to Abraham and defines a new sacred space with its own symbolic and practical implications."[35] So the OT concept of the land is transformed by Jesus into a new sacred space within a prophetic vision.[36]

Elmer Martens (2009) develops the concept of land as metaphor when using intertextual comparisons between OT and NT texts. He reaches similar conclusions as other recent studies regarding the transformation of the land from OT to NT but identifies metaphor as a primary vehicle when moving from OT to NT on the land theme.[37] A number of additional studies have developed various aspects of transformation to the land concept when moving from OT to NT.[38] Because of the scholarly interest in the land theme

---

31. Wright, *God's People in God's Land*, 111.
32. Wright, *God's People in God's Land*, 111.
33. Wenell, *Jesus and Land*, 139.
34. Wenell, *Jesus and Land*, 139.
35. Wenell, *Jesus and Land*, 139.
36. Wenell, *Jesus and Land*, 140–42.
37. Martens, "Reading the Earth Story," 226–32.
38. Additional studies which focus on the transformation of the land from OT to NT include T. Desmond Alexander, "Beyond Borders: the Wider Dimensions of the Land," in *The Land of Promise: Biblical, Theological, and Contemporary Perspectives*, 35–50 (2000); Adam Gregerman, "Comparative Christian Hermeneutical Approaches to the Land Promises to Abraham," in

in recent decades, this has also been developed in wider theologies of the OT[39] and the NT.[40]

The most significant developments in the literature for the purpose of this study are (1) the transformation from OT land to Christ himself in the NT;[41] (2) the widening of the Abrahamic promise to encompass the entire renewed earth in the age to come in the NT vision;[42] (3) the transformation and interrelationship between land and sword themes when moving from OT to NT.[43] What will also be further analyzed in this study is the NT communities as freely gathered communities of faith which are not based on land promises and how that impacts the transformation (and discontinuity) of the land theme when moving from OT to NT writings.

LITERATURE ON THE SWORD

A theme that is investigated for this study is the change that occurs when moving from the OT to the NT in regard to the use of the sword by God's people. The early church encountered difficulties with this issue; Marcion took issue with the violence in the OT and rejected the god of the OT. Over time, the church rejected Marcion's solution and affirmed the inspiration of the OT. Various church leaders defended the OT through the use of prophetic fulfillment themes or allegorical interpretation. Origen (d. 254) is well known as a pacifist and has been noted for his problematic allegorical interpretations of the OT. But in a substantive and decidedly non-allegorical statement, Origen defends Israel's use of the sword in the OT:

Cross Currents 64.3 (2014) 410–25; and Walter C. Kaiser Jr., "Israel and its Land in Biblical Perspective," in *The Old Testament in the Life of God's People: Essays in Honor of Elmer A. Martens*, 245–56 (2009).

39. cf. Waltke, *Old Testament Theology*, 512–87.
40. cf. Beale, *New Testament Biblical Theology*, 750–72.
41. Exemplified in Davies' early work, *Gospel and the Land*, 179; 367–70.
42. Exemplified in Dempster, *Dominion and Dynasty*, 3813–14.
43. Exemplified in Waltke, *Old Testament Theology*, 562.

in the case of the ancient Jews, who had a land and a form of government of their own, to take from them the right of making war upon their enemies, of fighting for their country, of putting to death or otherwise punishing adulterers, murderers, or others who were guilty of similar crimes, would be to subject them to sudden and utter destruction whenever the enemy fell upon them; for their very laws would in that case restrain them, and prevent them from resisting the enemy.[44]

In other statements, Origen defended Christian pacifism based on the teaching of Jesus in the NT. His position emphasized a sharp discontinuity when moving from OT to NT.[45]

The topic of violence (divinely sanctioned or otherwise) in the Bible has become a major focus of both scholarly[46] and popular writing. Since the focus of this study is the comparison between OT and NT texts and how the overall discontinuity is interpreted regarding the sword, this provides significant limits to the review of the literature. In the field of biblical theology, addressing this issue of continuity and discontinuity makes it necessary to trace overall biblical themes rather than creating a rigid separation between OT and NT theology. Willem VanGemeren notes that "the task of biblical theology concerns both the study and appreciation of the many themes of Scripture and their inner relationships."[47] This includes

---

44. Origen, *Contra Celsus*, 7:26

45. While Origen often used allegory when referring to OT battles, his position as noted above included a necessary and actual use of the sword by the nation of Israel.

46. Recent works include Frank Ritchel Ames and Brad E. Kelle, eds. *Writing and Reading War: Rhetoric, Gender, and Ethics in Biblical and Modern Contexts* (2008); Gregory A. Boyd, *Crucifixion of the Warrior God: Interpreting the Old Testament's Violent Portraits of God in Light of the Cross* (2017); Laura L. Brenneman and Brad D. Schantz, eds. *Struggles for Shalom: Peace and Violence across the Testaments* (2014); Paul Copan, et al., eds. *Holy War in the Bible: Christian Morality and an Old Testament Problem* (2013); Richard S. Hess and Elmer A. Martens, eds. *War in the Bible and Terrorism in the Twenty-First Century* (2008); and J. Harvey Walton and John H. Walton, *The Lost World of the Israelite Conquest: Covenant, Retribution, and the Fate of the Canaanites* (2017).

47. VanGemeren, "Systems of Continuity," 1147–48.

Searching For Answers

themes that continue from the OT to the NT but undergo significant change.

In *The Politics of Jesus: Vicit Agnus Noster* (1972) John Yoder contributed a significant work on the social and political relevance of Jesus in the contemporary world. He included analysis of the use of the sword in ancient Israel along with a discussion of Romans 13 and the use of the sword for the early church. In reviewing the OT in relation to war, Yoder emphasizes Israel's dependence on God[48] and His divine intervention.[49] He traces that attitude forward as something that would still have been part of the social fabric of Israel during the time of Christ and relates it to Jesus' preaching of the kingdom of God.[50]

Yoder also focuses on Romans 13 and examines this passage and its context from a pacifistic perspective. Linking Romans 12:19 and 13:4, Yoder interprets these passages to mean that "the function exercised by government is not the function to be exercised by Christians."[51] One problem is that Paul does not even directly address whether Christians can serve in government in Romans 12 and 13. Yoder seems to read his pacifism into his interpretation of Romans 13:1–7 to deny that government (in its proper function) has an actual God-given use of the sword.

In a positive direction, Yoder rightly criticizes proponents of just war theory for using Romans 13 to claim that Christians are duty-bound to obey the state and participate in the state's legally justified killing.[52] Proponents of just war theory have at times pushed their interpretation of Romans 13 in the matter of submission to government too far in this direction to claim that participation in war is a Christian duty, which Yoder rightly criticizes.[53] Romans 13 has been used to support corrupt regimes or to

---

48. The theme of Israel's dependence on God in battle was treated earlier in von Rad's *Holy War in Ancient Israel* (1958), 71–73. In this significant early work, von Rad analyzes the concept of Yahweh as warrior and "holy war" in the OT.

49. Yoder, *Politics of Jesus*, 76–84.

50. Yoder, *Politics of Jesus*, 84–85.

51. Yoder, *Politics of Jesus*, 198.

52. Yoder, *Politics of Jesus*, 193–94.

53. Yoder, *Politics of Jesus*, 203.

justify the church being in support of ungodly kings.⁵⁴ Since Paul does not address whether or not Christ's followers should serve in governmental functions in this passage, it has been incorrectly marshalled to claim that serving in the military or the police is a duty required of believers. The overall context of Romans 13 as well as other biblical examples mitigate against an absolute obedience to government.⁵⁵ Additional analysis of Romans 13 and its context will be included in the chapter on the sword.

Using an intertestamental and intertextual approach, Bruce Waltke traces the use of the sword from the OT into the NT and analyzes the change that takes place. Waltke examines the OT depictions of *I AM* as deliverer and warrior.⁵⁶ Divine involvement in warfare for Israel is analyzed in the Exodus, Joshua and Judges, and the monarchy. The alternative point is made that, when Israel becomes unfaithful, Yahweh becomes a warrior against Israel for the purpose of judgment and cleansing by utilizing Gentile nations against Israel.⁵⁷ While not downplaying the reality of OT warfare for the nation of Israel, Waltke also states that "an accredited method detects dispensational changes in God's role as warrior in the history of salvation."⁵⁸ He describes the transformation regarding the sword in the NT by saying that the battleground of the church is spiritual in nature and that "carnal weapons are renounced."⁵⁹ Various NT passages are cited to support the claim that the church "should never militarize"⁶⁰ but instead engage in spiritual warfare. Warfare will not cease until Christ returns and the earth is regenerated.⁶¹

Stephen Chapman analyzes OT warfare and the issue of "holy war" in Israelite history. Contrasts and similarities between the OT nation and the warfare in surrounding nations are described, and

---

54. Keener, *Romans*, 155–56.
55. Moulder, "Romans 13 and Conscientious Disobedience," 21–23.
56. Waltke, *Old Testament Theology*, 376–99.
57. Waltke, *Old Testament Theology*, 399–403.
58. Waltke, *Old Testament Theology*, 394.
59. Waltke, *Old Testament Theology*, 404.
60. Waltke, *Old Testament Theology*, 403.
61. Waltke, *Old Testament Theology*, 404.

SEARCHING FOR ANSWERS

the divine warrant for battle in OT texts is analyzed.[62] When moving from OT to NT, Chapman points out the change from physical battle to spiritual battle.[63] He describes the transformation by saying "the Old Testament contains no legitimate textual warrant at all for believers to shoulder arms and do physical battle with unbelievers in order to convert them or to conquer their territory."[64] He adds that "enemies are now to be loved (Matt 5:43-48) rather than fought. Taking up the sword is unproductive and self-defeating (Matt 26:52)."[65]

Elmer Martens examines peace and violence in the Bible and promotes the thesis that the message of the gospel is reconciliation and peace.[66] God's means of peace is the Cross, where "the incarnate Christ absorbed violence."[67] Human violence in the OT is traced back to the root cause of sin.[68] God's justice and holiness in the OT are identified as reasons for God's command to Israel to use the sword.[69] God as Warrior in the OT is examined, along with the transformation in the NT where "God the Warrior becomes God the martyr."[70] Christ engages in spiritual battle in the NT and defeats the powers of evil through the Cross.[71] It should be noted that W. H. Brownlee (1983) had earlier developed this transformation from OT holy war to NT martyrdom[72] and sees the suffering of Christ as a different form of warfare. Christ is still the divine warrior.[73]

The overall discontinuity regarding the use of the sword by God's people when moving from OT to NT is quite pronounced in the canonical texts but has been interpreted in a variety of ways. For

---

62. Chapman, "Martial Memory, Peaceable Vision," 52-59.
63. Chapman, "Martial Memory, Peaceable Vision," 63-66.
64. Chapman, "Martial Memory, Peaceable Vision," 63.
65. Chapman, "Martial Memory, Peaceable Vision," 66.
66. Martens, "Towards Shalom," 33.
67. Martens, "Towards Shalom," 34.
68. Martens, "Towards Shalom," 43.
69. Martens, "Towards Shalom," 46-50.
70. Martens, "Towards Shalom," 52-54.
71. Martens, "Towards Shalom," 54-55.
72. Brownlee, "Holy Martyrdom," 286-92.
73. Brownlee, "Holy Martyrdom," 286.

some, the uncomfortable issue of God commanding the destruction of the Canaanite tribes has been treated as a human rather than divinely directed warfare.[74] This naturally calls into question the divine inspiration of the OT. Another approach that accepts divine inspiration has been to treat some of the wording in Joshua as hyperbolic military language rather than literal language.[75]

Moving to the NT, some deny the transformation where Christ commands his followers to put away the sword and love their enemies. One approach is to claim that Christ was actually promoting violent rebellion against the Roman Empire and was therefore crucified.[76] Some scholars who discount the historical reliability of the NT documents take a similar approach, claiming that the later church transformed Jesus into a non-violent figure in order to curry favor with the Romans.[77] Some studies accept the divinely sanctioned use of war in the OT but point out limiting factors[78] and discuss reasons this no longer applies today.[79] This last option seems to be the most consistent with the presupposition of divine inspiration for both the OT and the NT, although there are many who have wrestled with the ethical and theological implications of the destruction of the Canaanite tribes.

While the OT nation is said to have been given divine authorization for the use of the sword, the NT communities were told (in the voice of Christ) to put away the sword (Matt 26:51–52; cf. John 18:34–38). In the NT, the sword that was once a physical sword becomes the sword of the Spirit. N. T. Wright points out that for Paul the battle has been redefined—it is now metaphorical and spiritual.[80] The battle shifts from Israel's battles as a nation in the physical realm to a battle against sin and death.[81]

---

74. Copan and Flannagan, *Genocide*, 39.
75. Copan and Flannagan, "Ethics of Holy War," 208–29.
76. Martin, "Armed and Not Dangerous," 3.
77. cf. Brandon, *Jesus and the Zealots*, 221–82.
78. Martens, "Toward Shalom," 33–57.
79. Copan and Flannagan, *Genocide*, 233–45; Yoder, *Politics of Jesus*, 86–88.
80. Wright, *Paul and the Faithfulness of God*, 31129.
81. Wright, *Paul and the Faithfulness of God*, 11096.

Jesus and the Sword

Jesus also comes under scrutiny in regard to the sword. Some have claimed that Jesus was really a proto–Zealot who was advocating the violent overthrow of the Roman government and was therefore crucified.[82] This approach has not convinced the majority of scholars,[83] primarily because of a lack of supporting evidence in the available historical sources. Jesus' debated statement on buying a sword in Luke 22 will be examined in greater detail, and various perspectives will be analyzed in the chapter on the sword.

N. T. Wright takes the position that the battle that Jesus was engaged in was not a military battle but a battle against evil and Satan; the revolutionary method of Jesus included suffering and the Cross.[84] Wright points out that the evidence does not support a militaristic version of Jesus and posits that Jesus was actually calling Israel to repent of nationalistic militarism in his teaching.[85] The widely held position that Jesus did not advocate the use of the sword in his preaching and example will be accepted for this study. A key point will be further analysis on the change between the OT nation and the NT communities of faith regarding the sword.

LITERATURE REVIEW ON THE TEMPLE

The theme of the temple undergoes major change when moving from the OT to the NT. The transformation is widely acknowledged by biblical scholars.[86] Davies noted the connection between

---

82. Brandon, *Jesus and the Zealots*.
83. Burge, *Jesus and the Land*, 622–29.
84. Wright, *Victory of God*, 465.
85. Wright, *Victory of God*, 450.
86. Contemporary writers who address this temple transformation include G. K. Beale, *The Temple and the Church's Mission: A Biblical Theology of the Dwelling Place of God* (2004); Daniel J. Hays, *The Temple and the Tabernacle: A Study of God's Dwelling Places from Genesis to Revelation* (2016); Paul M. Hoskins, *Jesus as the Fulfillment of the Temple in the Gospel of John* (2006); Craig S. Keener. "One New Temple in Christ," *AJPS* 12.1 (2009) 75–92; Nicholas Perrin, *Jesus the Temple* (2010); and N. T. Wright, *Jesus and the Victory of*

the land and the temple in the OT and analyzed how the temple theme is transformed in the NT.[87] T. Desmond Alexander traces the temple theme from OT to NT and identifies it as a major theme of biblical theology.[88] N. T. Wright analyzes the temple transformation in terms of symbol and worldview.[89] Paul's passages on the NT communities of believers as the temple of God (1 Cor 3:16-17; 2 Cor 6:14— 7:1; Eph 2:11-22) are widely acknowledged as evidence of the transformation of the temple theme in the NT.

The attitude of Jesus towards the temple has been widely debated in recent scholarship.[90] Was the action of Jesus in driving out the moneychangers a cleansing, or was it a prophetic parable of destruction? E. P. Sanders stated that there are "a few passages attributed to Jesus about Jerusalem and the Temple, all of them favorable."[91] He later acknowledges, however, that "sayings predicting or threatening the destruction of the temple are very deeply imbedded in the New Testament traditions about Jesus"[92] and that "Jesus' act of overturning the tables of the moneychangers should be understood in the light of these statements about the destruction of the temple."[93]

The scholarly continuum regarding Jesus' attitude towards the temple ranges from him being "overtly hostile (anti-temple) to being highly sympathetic (pro-temple)."[94] Nicholas Perrin identifies fourteen different scholarly viewpoints on what Jesus meant by the temple cleansing incident,[95] an amazing array of opinions. Fortunately, the background debate on what Jesus *might have meant* by the temple cleansing is not determinative for the focus of this study,

---

God, 405-38; 490-518 (1996).

87. Davies, *Gospel and the Land*, 94-104; 185-94.

88. Alexander, *Eden to the New Jerusalem*.

89. Wright, *Paul and the Faithfulness of God*, 2940-3292; *People of God*, 224-26; 409-10.

90. Wright, *Victory of God*, 413.

91. Sanders, "Jerusalem and Its Temple," 190.

92. Sanders, "Jerusalem and Its Temple," 191.

93. Sanders, "Jerusalem and Its Temple," 191.

94. Sweeney, "Temple," 612.

95. Perrin, *Jesus the Temple*, 89-91.

which is the wider picture of transformation from OT temple to NT communities of faith as seen in the completed canonical texts.

N. T. Wright analyzes the temple symbolism as it relates to the words and actions of Jesus.[96] He concludes that "Jesus saw himself, and perhaps his followers with him, as the new Temple."[97] Jesus seeing himself as the new temple can certainly be seen in the wording in John 2. Perrin reviews the background of John 2:19 and related passages and concludes that, "corroborated by the entirely credible passion predictions, John's report that Jesus publicly spoke of raising up the temple *and* publicly promised to do so in three days holds solid historical claim."[98] Paul Hoskins reviews the background and meaning of John 2:19 and states that "this suggests that Jesus' body is the replacement for the Jerusalem Temple, whose days are numbered as the special locus for the presence of God and for true worship (John 4:20-24)."[99] Being raised up in three days (John 2:19) clearly points to the resurrection of Jesus. Jesus' resurrected body as the beginning point of the NT transformation of the temple symbolism is acknowledged for this study.

While the early NT church does not reject the Jerusalem temple outright (Acts 3:1-10; 21:17-26), the adoption of temple language in the NT shows that the community of believers becomes the temple of God (1 Cor 3:16-17; 2 Cor 6:14-7:1; Eph 2:11-22). James Dunn surveys the NT documents regarding the transformation of the temple theme and identifies a uniform position that there was no longer a need for the temple.[100] Sacred space, the priesthood, blood sacrifices: all had been transformed.[101] A weakness in Dunn's perspective is his conclusion that Jesus' understanding of his death is unclear in relation to the sacrificial system.[102] This seems unlikely in light of a number of statements in the NT

---

96. Wright, *Victory of God*, 405-28.
97. Wright, *Victory of God*, 426.
98. Perrin, *Jesus the Temple*, 106.
99. Hoskins, *Jesus as Fulfillment*, 116.
100. Dunn, *Parting of the Ways*, 95.
101. Dunn, *Parting of the Ways*, 95.
102. Dunn, *Parting of the Ways*, 56.

documents (Matt 26:28; 20:28; Mark 10:45; 14:24; 1 Cor 11:23–26; John 6:51–66). How the transformation in the temple theme came about over time is a significant point of debate and analysis in the literature, but the end result is clear in terms of the adoption of a new temple symbolism in the NT.

While there is wide acknowledgement of the transformation regarding the symbolism of the temple from OT to NT, there is discussion about the degree to which the NT communities adapted the temple language to provide an alternative to the Jerusalem temple. Timothy Wardle proposes that the adoption of NT temple language has some similarities with other alternative temple movements, namely, "the Samaritan temple on Mount Gerizim, the Oniad temple in Leontopolis, and the "temple of men" at Qumran."[103] He suggests that "though the formation of each temple was a complex affair, in each case the primary motivating factor appears to have been conflict with the Jerusalem religious establishment."[104] Wardle posits that the NT temple language was a way to register dissent.[105] While this is possible, the much more radical step was the inclusion of the Gentiles in the new temple language.[106] In any case, the NT communities as the temple of God provided an alternative to the Jerusalem temple without necessitating the outright rejection of the Jerusalem temple. The change is very significant but less abrupt than an actual physical replacement for the temple.

The transformation of the temple theme in the NT also included key realities under the rubric of the temple. The themes of holiness, animal sacrifice, and the presence of God are all linked to the Jerusalem temple and undergo transformation in the NT. Marcus Borg claims that the emphasis on holiness as separation in Jewish thinking was being challenged by Jesus.[107] For Jesus, the temple was to be a house of prayer for all nations (Mark 11:17; Luke 19:46; Isa 56:7) and "if Israel persisted in the quest for holiness, he warned,

---

103. Wardle, *Temple and Early Christian Identity*, iv.
104. Wardle, *Temple and Early Christian Identity*, iv.
105. Wardle, *Temple and Early Christian Identity*, 333.
106. Wardle, *Temple and Early Christian Identity*, 338.
107. Borg, *Conflict, Holiness and Politics*, 209–11.

the temple would be destroyed by the imperial power which it was already confronting."[108] While Jesus was definitely challenging current practices regarding holiness as separation (cf. Luke 7:36–50; Matt 9:9–13), it would not necessarily follow that it is the rejection of Jesus' holiness paradigm (a paradigm of inclusion) that would result in the destruction of the temple.[109]

Barriers between Jews and Gentiles are removed so that they can dwell in unity in the new temple (Eph 2:8–22). Food laws, circumcision, and Sabbath laws are no longer required in the NT. This is a significant transformation. For the NT communities, the emphasis is separation from idolatry and sin itself while Jewish and Gentile believers are joined together through faith in Christ. In the NT temple, Gentiles were given "full and equal status in the temple community."[110] The former dividing wall of hostility has been broken down (Eph 2:14). According to Craig Keener, "Paul declares that this barrier, established by biblical laws dividing Jews from Gentiles, has been shattered by Jesus Christ (Eph 2:14–15)!"[111] All cultural distinctions between Jewish and Gentile believers were not erased; but through Christ these differences were transcended in a new unity.[112]

Animal sacrifice is no longer needed in the temple made up of Christ's followers because "the ultimate redemptive-historical purpose of the temple sacrifices was typologically to point to Christ as the ultimate sacrifice of himself, which he would offer for the sins of his people as a priest, at the Cross, and in the eschatological temple."[113] The change from animal sacrifice in the OT to Christ's sacrifice at the Cross is noted by too many authors to mention. It is one of the major areas of discontinuity between the OT and NT.

---

108. Borg, *Conflict, Holiness and Politics*, 211.

109. Borg later goes on to include the rejection of Jesus and his message as part of the quest for holiness (that is, the quest for holiness as separation), in *Conflict, Holiness and Politics*, 216–17.

110. Wardle, *Temple and Early Christian Identity*, 339.

111. Keener, "One New Temple," 79.

112. Karakolis, "Formation of the Pauline Communities," 376–78.

113. Beale, *New Testament Biblical Theology*, 632.

The presence of God that was closely identified with the OT temple becomes joined to the temple terminology for the communities of faith in Christ. Central to Paul's temple terminology "is the belief that the Holy Spirit now resides in the midst of the community in the same way that the presence of God was understood to dwell in the Jerusalem temple."[114] The presence of God by the Spirit was a reality in the NT temple of believers.[115] Ultimately the OT temple is replaced by the new, with Bruce Chilton noting that "the Epistle to the Hebrews spells out how Jesus' replacement of the temple is not simply eschatological but already accomplished and definitive."[116]

THREEFOLD DIVISION BETWEEN CIVIL, CEREMONIAL, AND MORAL LAW

It should be mentioned that a traditional explanation for a number of discontinuities between the OT and the NT is that the civil law and the ceremonial law have been fulfilled by Christ, but the moral law continues in the NT. This is an explanation cited in the Westminster Confession.[117] But scholars have pointed out that there are weaknesses in this explanation. Thomas Schreiner notes that "it does not sufficiently capture Paul's stance toward the law."[118] A significant difference in the NT is that the empowerment of the Spirit places believers in a different relation to the Law as compared to the OT.[119] It has also been pointed out that the civil laws often included a moral component as well.[120] Lastly, as an explanation for discontinuities between the OT and NT this three-fold explanation is limited to the rubric of the Law while there are various additional aspects of discontinuity between the OT and NT.

114. Wardle, *Temple and Early Christian Identity*, 307.
115. Wright, *How God Became King*, 247; Greene, "Spirit in the Temple," 742.
116. Chilton, "Temple, Jewish," 1181.
117. Schreiner, *Christians and Biblical Law*, 89.
118. Schreiner, *Christians and Biblical Law*, 89–90.
119. Fee, *People of God*, 100–101.
120. Schreiner, *Christians and Biblical Law*, 92.

The review of the literature supports the significance of this study, which analyzes the themes of land, sword, and temple in relation to the thesis. While these themes are widely treated in the literature, they are not analyzed as a whole in relation to the differences between God's instructions for a nation in the OT and His instructions for freely gathered communities of faith in Christ in the NT that are composed of Jews and Gentiles. This specific difference of vision between the canonical texts of the OT and NT can provide a method of contrast and points of investigation for further study. It is this method of contrast that will be the particular focus of the remaining chapters of this study.

3

A Methodology for Analyzing Change

A USEFUL METHODOLOGY FOR understanding continuity and discontinuity between the OT and the NT is the concept of intertextuality. There are different definitions of intertextuality,[1] making it crucial to define the concept carefully. The concept of intertextuality originated in literary studies in the 1960's.[2] Since it broadly included various ways that literary works quoted or referred to earlier literary works, it has had a number of uses. Some have developed intertextual methodologies that locate the meaning of the text in the present, in a reader-centered approach. That will not be the approach used here. Others have developed the concept of intertextuality in regard to the way later biblical texts refer to earlier ones, which is a central aspect of this study. Gary Schnittjer defines intertextuality as "the way in which later biblical writers rewrote, commentated on, reused imagery from, and otherwise dialogued with their scriptures."[3] According to Bruce

   1. Beale, *Handbook*, 40.
   2. Moyise, "Dialogical Intertextuality," 346–59.
   3. Schnittjer, *Torah Story*, 23–24. While Gary Schnittjer's primary focus is on the intertextual use of the Torah with later Scripture, he also highlights the way later writers such as David, the Gospel writers and Paul dialoged with earlier Scripture in a broader sense (24).

A Methodology for Analyzing Change

Waltke, "Intertextuality is the phenomenon whereby one passage of Scripture refers to another. Instances of intertextuality that involve an inner biblical exegesis, wherein later texts transform earlier ones by deepening, expanding, or revising them, best serve the task of biblical theology."[4] The correct usage of intertextual analysis also provides thematic connections that are necessary for understanding the whole of Scripture.[5]

This study will utilize the definitions of Gary Schnittjer and Bruce Waltke noted above, which are complementary to one another. OT biblical passages must first be interpreted in their immediate literary context and then related to the wider OT context and the later NT context in which they are used. An additional consideration is that NT writers are not only engaging in interpretation of OT texts; they are applying OT texts to the new situation, often in relation to Jesus as the Messiah.

Intertextuality in Relation to Literary Context

The literary context is basic for understanding the meaning of biblical texts and includes the surrounding words, sentences, paragraphs, and book. The literary context then widens to include other books by the same author, books from the same Testament, and the entire OT and NT.[6] The interpreter begins by discovering the author's intended meaning in a particular passage. The basic principle is that "each statement must be understood according to its natural meaning in the literary context in which it occurs."[7] This is a key concept since "literary context is at the heart of all language communication. It affects the reader's understanding of both the meaning of individual words and the meaning of the complete

---

4. Waltke, *Old Testament Theology*, 125. While Waltke refers to earlier parallel terminology used by other writers (125, ft. 27, 28) he is clearly developing his own definition of intertextuality here.

5. Waltke, *Old Testament Theology*, 126.

6. Blomberg et al., *Introduction to Biblical Interpretation*, 219.

7. Blomberg et al., *Introduction to Biblical Interpretation*, 217.

statement."[8] The wider literary context includes the pertinent Testament context and the entire biblical context.[9] It is these wider contexts in which intertextuality can play a key role.

Intertextual analysis investigates the way the initial biblical passage or concept is referred to in later passages in the OT and NT. The most obvious usage is direct quotations, such as restatements of earlier OT passages in later OT passages, or OT passages that are directly quoted in the NT. Scholars also identify allusions to OT passages that exist in the NT, and the allusions can be quite obvious, but can also move on a continuum from less obvious allusions all the way to distant "echoes."[10] As can be expected, there is wide consensus regarding direct quotations and obvious allusions that contain many related words and concepts, but less agreement the further one moves on the continuum towards distant "echoes" and faint allusions.[11] This study will focus on clear allusions that are widely recognized. At times, these quotes and allusions trace themes from the OT to the NT that address key issues regarding areas of discontinuity. In summary, a careful review of the literature regarding intertextuality in recent biblical theology has led to the conclusion that this is a useful methodology for analyzing discontinuity between the Testaments, as it has been defined and clarified above.

Intertextuality and Theological Interpretation

Simply tracing texts and allusions from the OT to the NT is insufficient to address the issue of continuity and discontinuity between the OT and NT. The NT writers engaged in theological interpretations of OT passages, and applied them to the new situation. This means that theological interpretation is often necessary to understand the way discontinuities between the OT and NT should be explained. So in addition to intertextuality, theological analysis will also be used in some cases to identify aspects of discontinuity. In some cases, there

8. Blomberg et al., *Introduction to Biblical Interpretation*, 218.
9. Blomberg et al., *Introduction to Biblical Interpretation*, 219.
10. Moyise and Oropeza, *Exploring Intertextuality*, 236–37.
11. Beale, *Handbook*, 31–35.

A Methodology for Analyzing Change

are clear allusions to OT passages in the NT, but the NT author goes further and gives commentary and interpretation which shows prophetic and/or conceptual fulfillment of OT passages.

In the forefront of the fulfillment theme was the recognition that Jesus was the Messiah who fulfilled many OT predictions. Donald Hagner notes that "Christianity is the goal and culmination of the story of Israel. Herein lies the *continuity*. For this reason, the biblical word 'fulfillment' is the perfect word to describe the situation."[12] While there is clearly continuity, Hagner goes on to say that "at the same time the extent of newness in the Gospels—and indeed the whole of the NT—is such that an unavoidable discontinuity with Judaism is caused."[13] Jesus is central to both the continuity and discontinuity between the OT and NT.[14]

Identifying and interpreting continuity and discontinuity between the OT and NT is a significant subcategory of biblical theology[15] which, of necessity, demands a biblical theology that encompasses both the OT and NT. This includes comparisons between OT and NT texts, as well as analysis of well documented allusions and themes. Since the thesis focuses on what is believed to be an explanation for many discontinuities, the concept of intertextuality provides a helpful methodology to make comparisons across the OT and NT. This methodology provides a fresh look at the problems rather than being bound by some of the limitations of older methods. Intertextuality will be carefully utilized as described above for the study, with the crucial goal of accurate interpretation of OT and NT concepts and passages.

---

12. Hagner, "Continuity and Discontinuity," 104.
13. Hagner, "Continuity and Discontinuity," 104.
14. Baker, *Two Testaments, One Bible*, 270–75.
15. Feinberg, *Continuity and Discontinuity*.

4

Changes Regarding the Land

A MAJOR AREA OF discontinuity that can be observed between the OT and NT is that the OT people of God become established on a specific land that is promised to them by God while the NT followers of Christ become established as freely gathered communities sprinkled among various nations. The NT records no territorial land promise given by God to these faith communities regarding this current age. This is a momentous shift and a remarkable demonstration of discontinuity between the OT and NT. The NT church was not established on land promises, but was established as communities of faith in Christ that would ultimately exist in all nations of the world, consisting of both Jews and Gentiles.

Intertextual comparisons between the OT and NT canonical texts themselves lead to evidences of a transformation: there is discontinuity concerning the land because the focus on land is transformed towards an eternal inheritance in the age to come (1 Pet 1:3–5; 1 Cor 15:50–53; Rom 4:13) and in the person of Christ who is the heir of all things (Heb 1:2). To further examine this discontinuity between the OT and NT canonical texts, it will be necessary to begin by focusing on the OT theology of the land.

The Old Testament Theology of the Land

Beginning in Genesis, the land is given great importance. God is identified as the sole creator of the land, the heavens, and all of creation (Gen 1:1-31). "He exists alone and creates solely as an expression of his own plan and purpose."[1] Before the fall of humanity, the Garden of Eden is established as a place for mankind to live and to have communion with God. This is the first use of land as a sacred space.[2] God walked in the garden in the cool of the day and interacted directly with the human beings he had created (Gen 3:8-10; 2:19). The Garden is the first sanctuary, and its land is blessed.[3] This Paradise is "a place without pain, without suffering; a time when love and peace flourish."[4] After the tragic disobedience of Adam and Eve, the ground is cursed and they are driven from the Garden (Gen 3:17-24). The curse on the ground and the curse of sin disrupts God's perfect creation, and the growing impact of sin upon humanity and the world is recounted beginning in Genesis 4. The narrative of the next seven chapters of Genesis describes an increasingly disruptive picture of the impact of sin upon humanity. Not only is there a curse upon the ground, but the initial corruption of humanity spreads to such an extent that the one God brings universal judgment on humanity through the flood (Gen 6:5—7:24). The land is purged, and Noah and his family begin anew with the Noachian covenant (Gen 9:1-17).

Abraham and the Promise of Land

Beginning in Genesis 12, God enacts a long term plan to restore humanity to himself. He does this by choosing and calling Abram (Abraham) and giving him a far reaching promise which has land as a key component:

---

1. Oswalt, "Theology of the Pentateuch," 852.
2. Martin, *Promised Land*, 37-38.
3. Martin, *Promised Land*, 38-39.
4. Waltke, *Old Testament Theology*, 248.

> Now the LORD said to Abram, "Go from your country and your kindred and your father's house to the land that I will show you. And I will make of you a great nation, and I will bless you and make your name great, so that you will be a blessing. I will bless those who bless you, and him who dishonors you I will curse, and in you all the families of the earth shall be blessed."[5]

Walter Kaiser notes that this was a threefold promise of seed, land, and a blessing that would impact all nations.[6] Abraham's descendants would become a nation and would inherit a land. The patriarchal promise is originally given to Abraham, further clarified to him, and later confirmed to Isaac and Jacob (Gen 12:1–3; 13:14–17; 17:7–9; 26:2–4; 28:13–15). Since it is Abraham's particular descendants who will become this great nation (Gen 12:2; 13:15–16; 17:7–8; 28:13–14), the ethnic identity of this nation is also clearly established. With these promises,

> four themes are clear: (a) Abraham will receive land as an everlasting possession; (b) Abraham's posterity will become a great nation in this place; (c) this promise is directly tied to the covenant; and (d) all of the people of the earth will be blessed by this promise. This promise of land and progeny is held up in the Old Testament as a remarkable gift of grace to Abraham and his descendants.[7]

When God establishes his covenant with Abraham (Gen 15:5–21), Abraham is told that his descendants would first be sojourners in another land and would be slaves there for four hundred years (Gen 15:13). Only after this delay would they be able to come back to the land of Canaan, because "the iniquity of the Amorites is not yet complete" (Gen 15:16). This delay is an indication that "God waited all during the days of the patriarchs, the days of the Egyptian bondage, and more, for the Canaanites to repent and turn away from the sins they had increasingly been heaping up against

---

5. Gen 12:1–3.
6. Kaiser, *Promise-Plan of God*, 54.
7. (Burge, *Jesus and the Land*, 181–84.

themselves."⁸ The iniquity of the Canaanite tribes, including the Amorites, is given as a theological justification for the fact that the land was going to be taken from them (Lev 18:24-28; Deut 9:1-5).

Nationhood and Land

The land promised to the patriarchs is stated as the reason that Yahweh is sending Moses to Egypt to bring the Israelites out of bondage and lead them to the land of Canaan (Exod 6:2-8). Through the exodus from Egypt, the distinctive identity of the Israelites as Yahweh's chosen nation is established (Deut 7:6-8; Exod 19:4-6), and under the leadership of Moses, the migration to the land of Canaan begins. The Mosaic covenant at Mount Sinai is Yahweh's covenant with the nation of Israel (Exod 19:1— 24:8) and "establishes them as 'a kingdom of priests and a holy nation' (Exod 19:6)."⁹ The Sinai covenant establishes boundary markers for the nation as God's people.¹⁰ Thus, nationhood, land, and covenant are linked together. Although the Israelites are temporarily on a journey through the wilderness, the land promise looms large since the patriarchal promise includes both land and the creation of a nation. Alexander notes that "since nationhood is normally understood as being a community of people sharing a common government and living in a clearly defined geographical region, possession of land is essential for Israel to become a 'holy nation.'"¹¹

Holiness and the Land

Since the land promised to Abraham was inhabited by the Canaanite tribes, Deuteronomy repeatedly stresses that the Canaanites would have to be conquered (Deut 11:22-25; 7:1-5; 9:1-3). W. D. Davies notes that, although the land at the time of the patriarchs was inhabited by the Canaanites, it "belongs to Yahweh and is his

8. Kaiser, *Promise-Plan of God*, 109.
9. Saucy, "Israel and the Church," 5033.
10. Christiansen, *Ritual Boundaries*, 44.
11. Alexander, "Beyond Borders," 42.

to dispose of, so that he can promise it to Abraham. This notion, that the land belongs to Yahweh himself, persisted throughout the Old Testament and beyond it."[12] Since the land belongs ultimately to Yahweh, what happens on the land is linked to an accountability to Yahweh. In Leviticus 18, after enumerating various sexual sins as well as idolatry, the statement is made, "Do not make yourselves unclean by any of these things, for by all these the nations I am driving out before you have become unclean, and the land became unclean, so that I punished its iniquity, and the land vomited out its inhabitants" (18:24–25). The defilement of the land is a key holiness concept which applies not only to the Canaanites, but to the Israelites as well:

> But you shall keep my statutes and my rules and do none of these abominations, either the native or the stranger who sojourns among you (for the people of the land, who were before you, did all of these abominations, so that the land became unclean), lest the land vomit you out when you make it unclean, as it vomited out the nation that was before you.[13]

Vomiting out its inhabitants is a form of personification; Davies notes that "the potency of the concept of the holiness of the land, though only derived from its relationship to Yahweh, emerges particularly in those passages which so forcibly and vividly personify the land."[14] The warning to the Israelites is that if they defile the land with idolatry, sexual sins, and other transgressions, the land would also vomit them out as it had the Canaanites (Lev 18:26–28). "The land is not a possession that may be enjoyed without reference to God. Possessing this land is contingent on Israel's ongoing faithfulness to God and obedience to his law. The land therefore is a byproduct of the covenant, a gift of the covenant. It is not a possession that can be held independently."[15]

---

12. Davies, *Gospel and the Land*, 27.
13. Lev 18:26–28.
14. Davies, *Gospel and the Land*, 30.
15. Burge, *Jesus and the Land*, 207–9.

Changes Regarding the Land

The establishment of a covenant nation on a physical land is crucial to understanding the historic life and vision of the nation of Israel. The land and the Sinai covenant provide specific boundary markers for the nation of Israel;[16] through a covenant relationship with Yahweh and obedience to the covenant teachings, a holy nation was to be maintained over time (Exod 24:3-8; Deut 31:10-13). Established in an ancient culture where polytheism, sexual corruption, violence, and injustice are widespread, Israel is to exist as a bounded community of covenantal holiness to testify to the uniqueness of the one God and his covenant teachings (Exod 19:5-6). Transmitting these truths over time would become a monumental challenge, and over time the polytheism, corruption, and false views of God in the Ancient Near East (ANE) would influence Israel to such an extent that Israel herself would have to go into exile (Amos 7:7-17; Jer 32:24-35).

Limits to the Land

There was not a vision of a worldwide military conquest of land by Israel in the OT. The promise of land to Abraham and his descendants, while given as a general statement in Genesis 12:1-3, is further clarified in Genesis 15 as a specific land inhabited by several tribes: "On that day the LORD made a covenant with Abram, saying, 'To your offspring I give this land, from the river of Egypt to the great river, the river Euphrates, the land of the Kenites, the Kenizzites, the Kadmonites, the Hittites, the Perizzites, the Rephaim, the Amorites, the Canaanites, the Girgashites and the Jebusites'" (15:18-21). This is also described as the land of Canaan in Genesis 17:8 when the statement is made to Abraham, "And I will give to you and to your offspring after you the land of your sojournings, all the land of Canaan, for an everlasting possession, and I will be their God." While some variations in the way the land promises are stated in the biblical texts have been debated, it is incorrect to say that this land would somehow continue to "expand with the

---

16. Christiansen, *Ritual Boundaries*, 44.

Freely Gathered Communities of Faith

increase and expansion of its inhabitants."[17] While not geographically precise in modern terms, there are specific boundaries for the land promised to Abraham and his offspring, upon which God promises to establish a nation. "Because the validity of the covenant is grounded in God's fidelity, the people's future existence rests in the hope of God's presence in a particular land provided by God, with geographical boundaries set by God."[18]

Since there were definite limits to the land that was promised to Abraham, the military campaign that would later take place to conquer the land would be limited in scope to "a relatively small portion of land (Canaan)—approximately the size of New Jersey."[19] Although the blessing promised to Abraham and his descendants would ultimately impact all the nations (Gen 12:3, 22:18), their military action was to be limited to a specific geographical "place." Israel was even prohibited from taking other specific lands:

> God prohibited Israel from conquering other neighboring nations such as Moab, Ammon, and Edom (cf. Deut 2:4, 9, 19; 23:7) because these people—not the Israelites—had legitimate title to their lands. God tells Israel not to provoke Edom to war, "for I will not give you any of their land, not even enough to put your foot on. I have given Esau the hill country of Seir as his own" (Deut 2:5).[20]

The promise of blessing for all nations was not used to justify world conquest through the use of the sword. T. D. Alexander clarifies that "while the borders of the Promised Land are set out in various passages with relative precision, there is no indication that Israel as a nation was to possess the whole earth."[21] The promise to Abraham that through his seed all nations would be blessed (Gen 22:15–18) indicated a worldwide impact for that blessing, but it was not to be accomplished through a worldwide military crusade. "Israel's national borders are never expected to extend to the ends

---

17. Martin, *Promised Land*, 74.
18. Christiansen, *Ritual Boundaries*, 33.
19. Copan and Flannagan, *Genocide*, 280.
20. Copan and Flannagan, *Genocide*, 62.
21. Alexander, "Beyond Borders," 43, ft. 21.

of the earth. For God's creation plans to be completed, other nations apart from Israel must also be included. Israel, however, has a special role to play *vis-a-vis* these nations."[22]

Robin Routledge notes regarding the Abrahamic covenant that "the central feature of the covenant is the divine promise *I will be their God* (Gen. 17:8)."[23] When God says "I will bless" (Gen 12:3; cf. 22:17), the covenant relationship with God is the foundation. The blessing does not occur in a vacuum. It "flows from Abraham's covenant relationship with God, and to share the blessing, the nations must also be brought to share the relationship. Thus the extension of divine blessing anticipates also the extension of the covenant relationship with God to all peoples."[24] It is not the territorial promise to Israel that should be expanded by references to "the nations" in the patriarchal promises (contra Williamson).[25] Rather, it is *through the means of* Abraham and his seed that these nations are to be blessed (Gen 22:18). Paul later accurately interprets the blessing of the nations through Abraham and his seed in a non-territorial way; this blessing, promised in Genesis 12:1–3, would be fulfilled through the gospel and the giving of the Holy Spirit to all who believe in Christ (Gal 3:2–9; 3:13–16). Only in the age to come would the transformed earth become liberated (Rom 8:19–25). However, for OT Israel, the land would play a key role in fulfillment of the promise to make Abraham a great nation.

Land Partitioning and Land Inheritance in the OT

The partitioning of the land of Canaan among the tribes of Israel is described in detail in Numbers 34. The apportionment passage is introduced by the statement, "This is the land that shall fall to you for an inheritance, the land of Canaan as defined by its borders" (Num 34:2). The land boundaries of the Israelite tribes are then given in some detail, and the point of emphasis is that each tribe

22. Alexander, "Beyond Borders," 43.
23. Routledge, *Old Testament Theology*, 166.
24. Routledge, *Old Testament Theology*, 167.
25. Williamson, "Promise and Fulfillment," 20–22.

is to retain its land and apportion it among the clans and families of that tribe. The tribes of Reuben and Gad had previously claimed their land inheritance on the east side of the Jordan (Num 34:13–15; 32:1–33).

Although the settlement of the land was gradual and there are various reconstructions of how this may have happened,[26] the land is shown to have been apportioned down to the clan and family level. Test cases are presented to emphasize that the land was to remain in perpetuity with the family unit (Num 27:1–11), and land could not pass from one tribe to another (Num 36:1–13). Christopher Wright notes that "legal and institutional protection of the inalienability of the land applied both to the 'father's house' and to the 'kin group.'"[27] The inalienability of the land was a key concept among the Israelites: "That the land should be held in the form of patrimonies which should not pass out of the family was a cherished idea in Israel that was protected by legislation and theologically justified and sanctioned."[28] The concept of land inheritance and inalienability was based on the idea that the land actually belonged to Yahweh, and therefore property could not be sold permanently outside of its original apportionment (Lev 25:23).[29] Abuses of land inheritance were addressed by OT prophets as matters of grave injustice (1 Kgs 21:1–27; Isa 5:8; Mic 2:1–2; Ezek 46:16–18).

The central point for this study is that the land is specifically apportioned. The land is a concrete reality, and this is expressed in the concept of inheritance since the land is passed down from fathers to their sons. The concept of land inheritance is a significant issue in OT Israel, and it is unethical for anyone, even kings, to interfere with the passing down of the family land (1 Kgs 21:17–19). While the concept of sons (or in some cases, daughters—Num 27:7–8) inheriting the physical land of their fathers is important in the OT, this is not specified in the NT for Christ's followers. Since the specific land promises of the OT are not applied to the

---

26. C. Wright, *God's People in God's Land*, 44–46.
27. Wright, *God's People in God's Land*, 57.
28. Wright, *God's People in God's Land*, 55–56.
29. Wright, *God's People in God's Land*, 58.

Changes Regarding the Land

NT communities as they expand into the Greco-Roman world, it is not surprising that the specific inheritance laws concerning the OT land are notably absent in the NT.

In the NT, land inheritance is widened from Israel inheriting the Promised Land to promises encompassing the whole world in the age to come (Rom 4:13; 2 Pet 3:10-13; 1 Pet 1:3-5; Rev 21:1-5). Stephen Dempster points out that "the burgeoning church composed of all nations is a fulfilment of the promise to Abraham, and the entire world is theirs for an inheritance, not just one country (Rom 4:13)."[30] The inheritance is not the physical land of the present age, but is an inheritance that is imperishable and kept in heaven for Christ's followers (1 Pet 1:3-5), although it will ultimately be fulfilled in a substantive and tangible way in the new heavens and new earth (2 Pet 3:10-13). The ultimate inheritor is Christ, who is called the heir of all things (Heb 1:1-2). Christ's followers are called fellow-heirs with Christ provided they suffer with him in order to be glorified with him (Rom 8:17).

Inheritance and the Kingdom of God

Rather than inheriting land in this life, the concept of inheritance is transferred to the kingdom of God in the NT (Matt 25:34; 1 Cor 6:9-10; 15:50; Gal 5:21). While there are various issues regarding the kingdom of God as taught in the NT, some basic features can be noted in regards to inheritance and the kingdom of God. The first is that flesh and blood cannot inherit the kingdom of God (1 Cor 15:50-58). In context, Paul's statement clearly points to the next life as the realm in which Christ's followers inherit the kingdom. So the inheritance of physical land in this life cannot be equated with inheriting the kingdom of God.

Paul's use of inheritance terminology "is a natural extension of the meaning of the Old Testament, which commonly refers to the land allotted to Israel."[31] The inheritance of Abraham is expanded to include the whole world. This means that "the entire world will

---

30. Dempster, *Dominion and Dynasty*, 3813-14.
31. Martin, *Promised Land*, 137.

become God's kingdom and his people's inheritance."[32] The ultimate inheritance of Christ is not the physical land of this present age but the renewed creation: "The idea of 'inheritance' is, as we have seen, important for Paul in connection with the Messiah: those who belong to him share the 'inheritance' which YHWH promised him in Psalm 2, namely the whole (renewed) creation."[33]

This ultimate inheritance can be seen most clearly in reference to Christ's fulfillment of the promises to Abraham. Christ is called the seed of Abraham, through whom all nations will be blessed (Gal 3:16; Gen 22:18). The promises to Abraham and his offspring ultimately include the inheritance of the entire world (Rom 4:13). This inheritance is not through the Law, but through faith in Christ (Rom 4:14–16; Gal 3:16–29). Through faith in Christ, one becomes an offspring of Abraham and an heir according to the promise (Gal 3:29). The blessing promised to Abraham has been extended to the Gentiles through faith in Christ (Gal 3:8). In Christ, the believer has obtained an inheritance (Eph 1:11), but there is no intimation that this inheritance is physical land obtained in the current age. The Holy Spirit is the guarantee of the believer's inheritance until full possession of the inheritance is realized (Eph 1:13–14).

The Prophets and the Land

Although the fulfillment of the divine promises regarding the land are a key dimension of Israel's identity as a nation in the OT, Israel's security in the land was based on faithfulness to the covenant. A significant shift takes place in that, after the height of expansion and consolidation that was achieved under David and Solomon, a decline begins. Solomon is led into idolatry through the influence of his many foreign wives, and this violation of the covenant is said to be the reason for the division of Israel into northern and southern tribes (1 Kgs 11:4–13). Here begins a long back and forth battle for the allegiance of the people to Yahweh, with the prophets in northern Israel and Judah calling the people to repentance and faithfulness to

---

32. Martin, *Promised Land*, 137.
33. Wright, *Paul and the Faithfulness of God*, 22760–61.

the Mosaic covenant. Idolatry and moral disobedience to the Mosaic Law would defile the land and endanger Israel's place on the land. Unfaithfulness to the covenant would have tragic consequences:

> The prophets interpret the invasions by Assyria (ca. 750–626 BC) and Babylon (605–586 BC) as the fulfillment of the covenant curses to purge the land: Israel is losing the land because she is abusing her usufruct just as the covenant curses had warned (Lev 26:34; Deut 28:64–68). Since the nation has destroyed her relationship with God, she also destroys her privilege to the land.[34]

If the land becomes defiled, it will ultimately reject its inhabitants (Lev 18:28; 20:22). The call to repentance is tied to continuation on the land. Without repentance, the result will be ejection from the land: "The latter prophets repeatedly demonstrate that God's punishment for Israel's disobedience to the covenant—and, more importantly, her covenant Lord—is exile and loss of land."[35]

The linkage of the sword to the land demonstrates an important twist in the prophetic writings, although it is illustrated all the way back to the period of the Judges: when Israel is unfaithful, Israel's sword will no longer avail to defend the land. This is because it is only with Yahweh's assistance that victories can be won, and Yahweh requires covenant holiness. If Israel becomes unfaithful, the promise of Yahweh's protection can be removed from the land and Israel will no longer be able to stand before its enemies (Amos 7:9–17; Jer 19:7; 32:24–28).

Exile from the Land, and Return to the Land

The destruction of northern Israel and the eventual exile of Judah are because the sword is now successfully wielded by Israel's enemies (Amos 7:9–17; Jer 19:7; 32:24–28). When God's nation departs from the covenant, it no longer has authority to successfully use the sword. Instead, God gives the prophets the power of

---

34. Waltke, Old Testament Theology, 831.
35. Martin, *Promised Land*, 99.

the prophetic word.[36] Because Israel has defiled the land, it must go into exile (Jer 16:9–18). However, the prophetic word purifies the remnant of God's people and prepares them to survive the exile.[37]

The prophets play a key role in providing hope in spite of the exile; they promise a return to the land. Robert Saucy notes that "of the sixteen canonical writing prophets, ten (Amos, Hosea, Isaiah, Micah, Zephaniah, Jeremiah, Ezekiel, Obadiah, Zechariah, Joel) write about a future restoration of Israel."[38] This prophetic hope, far from being later additions to the texts, provides actual guidance and genuine hope for a people who had been crushed by the exile.[39] So even though Israel experiences the painful and tragic loss of land and military defeat, the prophets play a key role by providing vision for a return to the land, a return from exile. The return from exile is a time of rebuilding, and Israel is assisted at this time by Gentile rulers. "The return from the exile was both a return to the city and to rebuild the temple; the temple became the center of both the religious and political life of the post-exilic community."[40]

Some scholars, notably N. T. Wright, have argued that the return from exile was not complete—it was not a complete fulfillment of the prophetic vision of the return from exile. The complete return from exile is then identified with aspects of Christ's ministry, but the impact of this return from exile is widened to include the nations.[41]

The prophetic vision in the OT goes far beyond the mere reestablishment of Israel on the land. The nations in the future are seen streaming to the "mountain of the Lord" (Mic 4:1–2); Gentiles are seen as being included in God's plan (Mic 4:2); physical alterations are seen as the wolf lies down with the lamb (Isa 11:6); and there is an ultimate vision of a new heavens and a new

---

36. Waltke, *Old Testament Theology*, 402.
37. Waltke, *Old Testament Theology*, 402.
38. Saucy, *Dispensational and Non-Dispensational Theology*, 223 n.6.
39. Waltke, *Old Testament Theology*, 401–2.
40. Davies, *Gospel and the Land*, 152.
41. Wright, *Victory of God*, 447–539; Wright, *People of God*, 268–389.

earth (Isa 65:17; 66:22). Summarizing this wider vision from a NT perspective, Waltke states that

> the prophets' predictions embrace a beginning of fulfillment in Israel's restoration from the exile, a victorious fulfillment in the church age stretching from Christ's first advent to his Parousia, and a consummation in the eschatological new heaven and earth when Christ's kingdom becomes coextensive with the creation.[42]

The Land Transformed in the New Testament

In the NT, the role of the land is greatly altered. Robertson notes that "the land which was once the specific locale of God's redemptive working served well within the old covenant as a picture of Paradise lost and promised. Now, however, in the era of the new-covenant fulfilment, the land has expanded to encompass the cosmos."[43] Rather than being bound to a specific portion of land on the earth, the NT people of God are promised eternal life through faith in Christ, and the *ultimate* inheritance of a transformed earth. This is clearly indicated as a future state since "according to his promise we are waiting for new heavens and a new earth in which righteousness dwells." (2 Pet 3:13; cf. Isa 65:17; 66:22). In the NT, there is no suggestion that Christians should "assume *for themselves* the land promises given to the patriarchs."[44]

Jesus and the Land

Burge notes that "Jesus is surprisingly silent with regard to the territorial aspirations and politics of his day."[45] Jesus only makes one direct reference to inheriting the earth or land in Matthew 5:5 (cf. Ps 37:11), and this should be interpreted as an eschatological

---

42. Waltke, *Old Testament Theology*, 824.
43. Robertson, "New Covenant Perspective," 139.
44. Burge, *Jesus and the Land*, 2377.
45. Burge, *Jesus and the Land*, 623–33.

reference to the meek inheriting the earth rather than any kind of land promise in the present age.[46] In context, the inheritance Jesus was speaking of in Matthew 5:5 was eschatological.[47]

To the twelve, Jesus says, "Truly, I say to you, in the *new world* (Greek παλιγγενεσία, translated *regeneration* in the NASB), when the Son of Man will sit on his glorious throne, you who have followed me will also sit on twelve thrones, judging the twelve tribes of Israel" (Matt 19:28). This should be interpreted as an eschatological reference to judgment at the end of the age. Although there are hints in this passage regarding land on a regenerated earth, this is clearly for the future age and is not an establishment of OT land promises for the disciples of Christ in the present age.

It may be objected that the reason the land promises are not stressed in the NT is that Israel was already in the Promised Land. Therefore, the land promises were not stressed in the ministry of Jesus and the apostles. While this has an initial appearance of plausibility, there are a few problems with this assertion. First, and most obviously, the nation of Israel was not in control of the land at the time of Christ. The Romans were in control, and Israel was a subject state. So, to truly gain control of the Promised Land, Israel would have to throw off the Roman yoke and gain independence. This would mean taking up the sword and engaging in battle with the Romans, something that Jesus and his later followers clearly did not advocate. So Jesus' lack of emphasis on the OT land promises likely points in another direction. Jesus avoided focusing on the territorial aspirations of Israel, and instead proclaimed the kingdom of God, a kingdom that is non-territorial in terms of taking land. It is only at the end of the age that Christ's followers would receive their inheritance (Matt 25:31–46).

Jesus demonstrates a freedom from territorial aspirations for the present age. To one who wished to follow him, Jesus replied, "foxes have holes and birds of the air have nests, but the Son of Man has nowhere to lay his head" (Luke 9:58; Matt 8:20). This statement reflects a complete disconnect with territorial ambition in the

---

46. Beale, *New Testament Biblical Theology*, 756–57.
47. Ladd, *Theology of the New Testament*, 450.

present age. There would be no territorial conquest; the itinerant ministry of Jesus was to keep moving—preaching, teaching, and healing from one place to another. There is no sense that he and his followers sought to gain control of a town or city, from which to conquer further territory. *The Son of Man has nowhere to lay his head*; this poignant statement highlights the separation of Jesus from the territorial and political aspirations of the day, and even a separation from the normal human aspirations of having a "place" of security.

To take this a step further, one can ask if Jesus even had the somewhat insecure "place in the land" that the typical Judean had in those days. It seems not, from the statement of Jesus about foxes having holes and birds of the air having nests. In an expression of political and religious power, the religious leaders and the Romans acted to take Jesus off the land. The crucifixion completely removed Jesus' right to live in the land. It was the most complete expression of religious and political power that could be accomplished. Although death took Jesus off the land, the apostles realized that his resurrection had established him as the cornerstone (Acts 4:10-12). The stone that was rejected by the builders had become, through Christ's resurrection, the cornerstone of the people of God (Ps 118:22; Matt 21:42; Acts 4:11).

As the early believers established communities of faith in the Greco-Roman world, there was no proclamation of new land promises for these communities. Nor was there a call to take land by the sword. Instead, the emphasis was on the kingdom of God and the proclamation of the death and resurrection of Jesus as Messiah and Lord (Luke 24:45-49; Acts 28:23-31; 20:25; Luke 8:1; 2 Tim 4:1-2). The preaching of the kingdom of God would not be limited to the land of Israel, but would include a witness to all nations (Acts 1:8; 28:30-31). Rather than a call to seize new lands, the gospels conclude with Christ's commission to make disciples of all nations (Matt 28:18-20), to preach the gospel to all (Mark 16:50), and that "repentance and forgiveness of sins should be proclaimed in his name to all nations, beginning from Jerusalem" (Luke 24:45-49).

The disciples' question for the risen Christ in Acts 1:6, "Lord, will you at this time restore the kingdom to Israel?" is a question which reflects that Jewish national aspirations were still in the thinking of the disciples at that point. Jesus indicated that it was not for them to know the times fixed by the Father (Acts 1:7); instead, they were to focus on the mission of witnessing to Christ "in Jerusalem and in all Judea and Samaria, and to the end of the earth" (Acts 1:8). The focus in Acts then gradually shifts from Israel to Asia, the European continent, and Rome. While there are many additional nuances that can be explored regarding Jesus and the Jewish aspirations of his day,[48] he clearly does not establish the OT land promises as a focus for his disciples.

Eternal life through faith in Christ is central to the NT (John 6:40-47; Acts 13:46-48; Matt 25:31-46; 1 Tim 1:15-16). While there are glimpses of eternal life in the OT (2 Kgs 2:8-12; Gen 5:22-24), eternal life through faith in Christ becomes the explicit doctrinal revelation of the NT (2 Tim 1:9-10). Eternal life as the inheritance of Christ's followers includes the realm of a transformed heaven and earth, rather than the current land and the fallen world system which has been corrupted by sin.

The Land Fulfillment in Christ

In the NT, there is no land conquest by the disciples, and the OT emphasis on the land is transformed to a Christ-centered vision. The believer's place "in Christ" becomes the focus instead of the OT Promised Land."[49] "In Christ" becomes one of Paul's most common terms, and it is "in Christ" that God's blessing is given in fulfillment of the promise to Abraham. According to Paul, at the Cross "Christ redeemed us from the curse of the law by becoming a curse for us—for it is written, "Cursed is everyone who is hanged on a tree"—so that *in Christ Jesus* the blessing of Abraham might come to the Gentiles, so that we might receive the promised Spirit through faith" (Gal 3:14-15). The blessing of the Spirit encompasses the Jews and Gentiles in every land who believe in Christ Jesus. Jesus is identified as the seed of Abraham, the One through whom God's

48. Walker, "Land and Jesus Himself," 101-18.
49. Cotton, *Studying the Old Testament*, 74.

blessing would come to the nations (Gal 3:13-16). Paul "universalizes faith in Christ in order to include all people; Paul universalizes the promises to Abraham in order to include all lands."[50]

Those who believe are blessed with every spiritual blessing in the heavenly places in Christ (Eph 1:3). This locates the promised blessing of Christ the Messiah in the heavenly realms, although it also leads to transformation in the age to come. Because of his sacrificial death, resurrection, and ascension, Jesus has been exalted to the right hand of God in the heavenly realms (Acts 2:33). His rule as Messiah has already begun in the heavenly realms, and through faith in Jesus as Messiah, those who believe are included "in Christ." Christopher Wright notes that

> by incorporation into the Messiah, all nations are enabled to enter upon the privileges and responsibilities of God's people. Christ himself takes over the significance and function of the land kinship qualification. "In Christ," answering to "in the land," denotes a status and a relationship, a position of inclusion and security, a privilege with attendant responsibilities.[51]

Christ's rule in the heavenly realms has a direct impact and tangible results in the present life through the impartation of the Spirit. The gift of the Spirit fulfills the promise of blessing made to Abraham that would impact all the nations (Gal 3:13-14). Love, joy, peace, righteousness, empowerment, and other dimensions of the Spirit's rule all find expression through Christ's followers and the ministries they fulfill in this world (Gal 5:22-23; Acts 1:8; Rom 14:17).

Paul and the Promised Land

Paul does not apply the OT land promises for Israel to the NT communities of faith in any direct or physical way. Regarding this lack of references to the Promised Land of Israel, N. T. Wright notes that "the reason the symbol of land appears to be almost entirely missing

---

50. Burge, *Jesus and the Land*, 1788-89.
51. Wright, *God's People in God's Land*, 111.

in Paul is that it has been swallowed up in a much larger element of symbolic praxis. Paul's mission was aimed precisely at declaring the Messiah, Jesus, as the world's true Lord, summoning people everywhere to believing allegiance to him."[52] The focus has changed to the ultimate inheritance of Christ, which is the entire transformed world. This transformed world is not gained by Christ's followers through physical conquest or taking physical territory, but only takes place at the Parousia:

> For Paul, God's kingdom—as we see clearly enough in 1 Corinthians 15.20-28—is not a non-material, post-mortem destination, but is rather the sovereign rule of the creator over the entire created order, with death itself, that which corrupts and defaces the good creation, as the last enemy to be destroyed. In other words, the final 'kingdom of God' is the whole world, rescued at last from corruption and decay, and living under the sovereign rule of God, exercised through the Messiah's people.[53]

In Romans 4:13, Paul writes that "the promise to Abraham and his offspring that he would be heir of the world did not come through the law but through the righteousness of faith." Here Paul states that Abraham would be "heir of the world," a specific expression that is not used in any of the Abrahamic promises in the OT, but in an intertextual comparison between the Abrahamic promises (Gen 15:18-21; 17:8; 22:15-18) and Romans 4:13, Paul's statement should be seen as an interpretation of the ultimate purpose of the Abrahamic blessing. Note the important distinction in the Abrahamic promises: Israel was promised a specific land, the land of Canaan (Gen 15:18-21; 17:8). This was a land with specific boundaries. Their nation was small by modern standards. But the promise to Abraham was also that, in Abraham's seed or offspring, all nations would be blessed (Gen 22:15-18). Since Paul later interprets this blessing as being fulfilled in Christ and the giving of the Holy Spirit (Gal 3:8-14), there is a worldwide impact that Paul sees through Christ and the gospel which leads to the blessing of the

---

52. Wright, *Paul and the Faithfulness of God*, 11036.
53. Wright, *Paul and the Faithfulness of God*, 11027.

nations. Paul clearly does not see land conquest by Christ's followers as the fulfillment of the promise to Abraham!

Looking at Romans 4:13 in the wider context of Paul's theology, Abraham becoming the heir of the world would take place through the Messiah and the ultimate inheritance of the entire renewed earth by the Messiah rather than by the land conquests of God's people.[54] The Messiah brings the promised blessing to all the nations of the earth, and inclusion in the "children of Abraham" through faith in Christ (Gal 3:7-9; 26-29) would include all of the followers of the Messiah in the inheritance of the Messiah. Describing this inheritance in connection to Romans 4:13, N. T. Wright points out that

> The Messiah will 'inherit' the earth, as Psalm 2 proclaimed, and the Messiah's people will share that inheritance. Romans 4.13 thus looks ahead, within the complex argument of the letter, to the majestic prophecy of 8.17-30, in which 'the inheritance' will indeed be 'the world', but the world renewed, reborn through the coming convulsion of birth-pangs.[55]

Commenting on the implications of Romans 4:13, Gary Burge states that

> Romans 4:13 is the only place where the apostle refers explicitly to the promises for the land given to Abraham and in this case Paul fails to refer to Judea. Paul writes that the promise to Abraham indicates that the patriarch would inherit the world (Gk *kosmos*). The universalizing intent of Paul has now shifted from the Gentiles to the domain of Gentile life. In Genesis Abraham was to inherit the Holy Land. In Romans 4.13, his claim is on the world.[56]

In the wider OT context, the purpose of Abraham's calling is seen as God's answer to the failure of Adam and Eve in the Garden.[57] The corruption and evil resulting from human sin is answered by

---

54. Gundry, *New Testament*, 584.
55. Wright, *Paul and the Faithfulness of God*, 11017.
56. Burge, *Jesus and the Land*, 1651-54.
57. Martin, *Promised Land*, 48.

the initiation of the divine, long range plan for the restoration of humanity. Abraham's seed and the promise of blessing that would impact all the nations provide the divine solution to the failure of Adam,[58] and Paul sees Messiah Jesus as the fulfillment of the promise made to Abraham that would provide this ultimate solution (Gal 3:13–29). The solution is not obtaining physical territory but faith in Christ and the gift of the Spirit.

THE SIGNIFICANCE OF THE LAND

While the land promises of the OT are greatly transformed in the NT, this does not negate the significance of the land of Israel for the Christian faith. Because of the Incarnation the land of Israel has a deep meaning.[59] In the analysis of Davies, the NT "personalizes 'holy space' in Christ, who, as a figure of history, is rooted in the land; he cleansed the Temple and died in Jerusalem, and lends his glory to these and to the places where he was, but, as Living Lord, he is also free to move wherever he wills."[60]

The land of Israel contains well known evidences of biblical places, events, and people. From the Dead Sea scrolls to the various artifacts, monuments, and inscriptions that have been uncovered, evidences for the authenticity of the biblical record are linked to the land. In this important respect, as a place of historical evidence, the biblical texts remain connected to the land.

The Ultimate Vision for the Land

While rooted in history, the NT vision ultimately culminates in God's grand purpose of reclaiming the entire created order, and this happens not through people claiming physical territory but through God's own intervention. Revelation summarizes this future divine intervention by saying, "The kingdom of the world has become the kingdom of our Lord and of his Christ, and he shall reign forever

---

58. Burge, *Jesus and the Land*, 1656–59.
59. Davies, *Gospel and the Land*, 366.
60. Davies, *Gospel and the Land*, 367.

CHANGES REGARDING THE LAND

and ever" (11:15). Peter Walker describes the wide sweep of God's purposes regarding the land:

> The call to Abraham (Gen 12) is the divine answer to the sin of Adam (Gen 3), and the election of Israel always has the ultimate goal of the blessing of the nations (Gen 12:3). The focus on the land of Israel was effectively a bridgehead within God's long-term purpose of reclaiming the *whole world* to himself and of bringing in his 'new creation', the restored Eden.[61]

Rather than a temporal land inheritance in this life for the people of God, it is the ultimate inheritance that comes into focus in the NT: a new heavens and a new earth (2 Pet 3:10–13); the New Jerusalem descending from heaven (Rev 3:12; 21:2, 10); and the actual presence of God in the city (Rev 21:22). It is through faith in Jesus as the Messiah that eternal life will become a reality in these environs (John 3:16). Christ's resurrection guarantees a resurrection body for those who believe (1 Cor 15), so the ultimate inheritance is not merely spiritual; it includes a transformed earth, the New Jerusalem, and the resurrection body. Concerning the OT land promises, Beale argues that "the physical way that these land promises have begun fulfillment is that Christ himself introduced the new creation by his physical resurrection."[62]

SUMMARY ON THE LAND

A change in divine strategy is seen in the major shift from one nation in the OT to freely gathered communities of faith in Christ in the NT. In the Torah, the OT nation was tied to a land; the NT communities of faith are *not* tied to one specific land. Since NT communities were freely gathered and were composed of Jews and Gentiles based on faith in Christ, they would not be founded on promises of land (as was the nation of Israel). NT communities would be formed in many nations. There is a major shift in that land possession (as a community) is not a religious requirement for the NT people of God.

61. Walker, "Land and Jesus Himself," 116.
62. Beale, *New Testament Biblical Theology*, 751.

NT communities were not founded on possession of a promised land in the current age. Instead, the vision of land is transformed to encompass Christ as the inheritor of all things and the ultimate inheritance that Christ's followers worldwide will share with him in the new heavens and new earth (Heb 1:1-2; Rev 11:15; 21:1-5).

As has already been seen, nationhood and land are linked together in the OT. Because Israel is a nation its land is a major focus both in terms of divine promises for obtaining the land and the divine requirements for staying on the land. The NT looks forward to the ultimate inheritance of the earth through Christ in the age to come, but this is brought about by the return of Christ and the direct intervention of God's apocalyptic judgment.

Looking forward to the additional themes to be traced in this study, the land change from OT to NT is also linked to other major areas that undergo transformation in the NT. In the OT the use of the sword is given divine authorization to obtain and protect the nation's land, while there is no divine authorization for the NT disciples to use the sword to obtain land in the NT. In the OT, the temple is linked to the land as well. The physical temple is the focal point of God's presence among God's people in the nation. In the NT, the temple emphasis is transformed and over time becomes a symbol for Christ as well as the community of believers (John 2:17-22; 1 Cor 3:16; 2 Cor 6:16-18).

The promise of land is also linked to the ethnic composition of the nation of Israel in the OT. The promise of land goes back to Abraham, and the people established on that land are to be his particular descendants through Isaac and Jacob which means that the cultural and ethnic distinctions of the people of God in the OT are linked to the issue of land as well. When Gentiles are welcomed as followers of Christ, ethnic barriers are removed, and the blessing of the nations promised through Abraham is seen as being fulfilled in the message of Christ and the reception of the Holy Spirit. The ways that these discontinuities between the OT and NT take place will be explored in the following chapters. If the focus of this study is correct, then the move from one nation in the OT to the NT communities of faith in Christ will explain many of the discontinuities between the OT and NT.

5

Changes Regarding the Use of the Sword

The Sword and the Land

Israel's use of the sword in the OT is connected to the provision of land. The land is a major focus of the Pentateuch, and the land promises to the patriarchs provide the backdrop for Israel's movement towards Canaan. Through the Exodus and the covenant at Sinai, Israel becomes established as God's holy nation (Exod 12—20; 19:6). Beginning with the journey through the wilderness and proceeding to the eventual entry of Israel into the land of Canaan, the use of the sword by God's people is given divine sanction (Exod 17:8–13; Deut 20:10–18). The association of a nation's god with military battle was common in the Ancient Near East: "Most ANE nation-states related war (in some way) to the activity of the divine, and so war as a concept could not be dissected from the rest of life in terms of "sacred" and "secular," as do many modern Western people."[1] Although the nation of Israel is said to have been given the use of the sword, it is repeatedly emphasized that only God's help will suffice to bring them victory in battle. The sword and military

1. Thomas, "A Neglected Witness," 69.

strength are not sufficient in themselves.² The promise of land and the use of the sword to obtain and defend that land are concepts that are linked, beginning in the wilderness, and extend into the period of the kings (cf. Num 32:1-22; 1 Kgs 20:1-22).

Uses of Force in the OT Nation

In the OT, there are three main distinguishable uses of lethal force by Israel which are tied to its nationhood and its land: a unique (and controversial) divine authorization to conquer the land of Canaan (Deut 7:1-5; 20:16-18); the use of the sword for national defense (Exod 17:8-16; 1 Sam 7:3-13); and the use of lethal force to enforce some of its societal laws (Exod 22:18-20; Lev 20; Deut 22:22). While the OT nation of Israel uses the sword in these ways, the NT church does not. A crucial point here is that, since the OT people of God were established as a nation on a specific land, they were given the use of the sword in relation to that land. But since the NT church was established as freely gathered communities which would ultimately exist in every nation, they would have neither land promises nor the use of the sword to obtain or protect "land." This is a massive shift, with numerous implications in history and in today's world.

A noteworthy limitation is that Israel was not said to have been given the use of the sword for a worldwide military conquest. The limits of the land were identified, however imprecisely by modern standards, as the lands encompassed by the patriarchal land promises (Gen 15:18-21; 17:8). Additional boundary features are described as the Israelites prepare to enter the land of Canaan (Num 34). Deuteronomy also recounts that Israel was forbidden to take the nearby territories of the Ammonites and the Moabites (Deut 2:4, 5, 9, 19; 23:7).

While there have been a number of recent studies highlighting the importance of the land in the OT and how the land theme is greatly altered in the NT, the linkage of the sword to the land is often not considered in current studies.³ It is significant that not only is the

2. Waltke, *Old Testament Theology*, 395-99.
3. For example, see T. Desmond Alexander, *From Eden to the New*

theology of the land greatly altered in the NT; the theology of the sword is also dramatically changed. The OT nation of Israel was given the use of the sword to obtain and defend its land; the NT church no longer has divine land promises (at least in this present age), but instead is to exist as freely gathered communities of faith in all nations of the world. The NT church would no longer have a divine sanction for the use of the sword; the church would not take territory or advance itself through the use of force. "The nation of Israel had armies; the church does (or ought) not have forces for waging war."[4]

While the OT land is identified as a specific region, the use of the sword is not specified in the patriarchal promises themselves. But the nation of Israel is given explicit divine authorization for the three uses of lethal force that were stated above, including the taking of the land of Canaan that is the focus of the patriarchal promises. Land, nation, and sword are consistently linked together.

New Testament Uses of the Sword

The three uses of the sword in the OT can be contrasted with the lack of use of the sword by the church in these areas in the NT:

1. As an offensive weapon for gaining land: The NT gives no authorization for the church to take physical territory or to advance the gospel through the use of force.

2. As a defensive weapon when attacked by enemies: In the NT church, believers flee from persecution rather than defending themselves with the use of the sword (Acts 8:1–4; 14:1–7).

Jerusalem: An Introduction to Biblical Theology (2008); Gary M. Burge, *Jesus and the Land: The New Testament Challenge to "Holy Land" Theology* (2010); the authors in *The Land of Promise: Biblical, Theological, and Contemporary Perspectives*, eds. Philip Johnston and Peter Walker (2000); and Oren R. Martin, *Bound for the Promised Land: The Land Promise in God's Redemptive Plan* (2015). These works do not address the issue of the sword in relation to the land. *An Old Testament Theology: An Exegetical, Canonical, and Thematic Approach* by Bruce K. Waltke with Charles Yu (2007) does include aspects of the sword in relation to the OT land and the NT in its wider treatment of various aspects of OT Theology (395–404).

4. Demarest and Lewis, *Integrative Theology* (vol. 3), 339.

The church itself has no divinely promised land to defend by use of the sword.

3. For enforcing societal laws: In the NT, the sword is never used by the church to punish those who violate biblical commands. For example, specific sexual sins are not punished by the death penalty in the NT church as they were in the OT (Lev 20:10–13; Deut 22:22). Instead, the church has only the power of excommunication: to remove someone who persists in sexual sin, through a process of church discipline (1 Cor 5:9–13; 5:1–2). This is because the church is a freely gathered community of faith, not a nation. Contra the theonomic position represented by Greg Bahnsen,[5] specific OT death penalties for specific crimes and sins cannot be forced upon the Gentile nations today because the NT church has no mandate to do so. There has only been one theocratic nation.

To examine key reasons for the changes regarding the sword, it will be necessary first to consider the impact of Jesus and his teachings in the NT.

Jesus and the Use of the Sword

While there are aspects of the kingdom of God that are debated,[6] the teaching of Jesus on the kingdom of God clearly did not advocate a physical kingdom of this world to be advanced through land conquests or the use of the sword. The relationship between the kingdom of God and the use of the sword by Christ's followers is brought out clearly in the Gospel of John, where Jesus tells Pilate,

> "My kingdom is not of this world. If my kingdom were of this world, my servants would have been fighting, that I might not be delivered over to the Jews. But my kingdom is not from the world." Then Pilate said to him, "So you are a king?" Jesus answered, "You say that I am a king. For this purpose I was born and for this purpose I have come into

---

5. Bahnsen, "Theonomic Reformed Approach," 132–43.
6. Kaiser, "Spiritual and National," 6043–265.

Changes Regarding the Use of the Sword

the world—to bear witness to the truth. Everyone who is of the truth listens to my voice." Pilate said to him, "What is truth?" After he had said this, he went back outside to the Jews and told them, "I find no guilt in him."[7]

This and other NT passages taken together clearly establish that the kingdom of God was not to be based on territorial conquest or the use of the sword (Matt 26:51–52; Luke 17:20–21; 18:15–17; 1 Cor 15:50; Acts 19:8–10; 28:23–31). Christ "never presented himself as an earthly king ruling over a restored, political state."[8] There are those who have tried to establish that Jesus was a proto-zealot who advocated armed rebellion against Rome and was therefore crucified, but Burge notes that this view has not been sustained by the data that is available about Jesus' teaching and ministry.[9]

It is significant that Matthew's Gospel with its Jewish focus also brings out the fact that Jesus repudiated the use of the sword. When soldiers came to arrest Jesus in the garden of Gethsemane a disciple "drew his sword and struck the servant of the high priest and cut off his ear. Then Jesus said to him, 'Put your sword back into its place. For all who take the sword will perish by the sword'" (Matt 26:51–52). "For all who take the sword will perish by the sword" is given as a principled statement of Jesus with universal significance. Citing this passage, Waltke notes that "the New Testament never defines the mission of the church by conquest of land or money or people. Its mission is to encourage the free submission of souls to the will of God that recognizes the dignity of all human beings as bearers of God's image. Carnal weapons are renounced (Matt 26:50–56; 2 Cor 10:4–5)."[10] Jesus forbids his disciples from using the sword to prevent his arrest (Luke 22:47–53; Matt 26:50–51; John 18:4–12), and he never advocated the use of the sword to spread Christianity. The teaching of Jesus on loving one's enemies and avoiding retaliation must also be cited in support of the non-violent emphasis of Jesus (Matt 5:38–48; Luke 6:27–36).

---

7. John 18:34–38.
8. Waltke, "Kingdom Promises," 5591.
9. Burge, *Jesus and the Land*, 622–53.
10. Waltke, *Old Testament Theology*, 403–4.

Luke 22:35-38 and the Use of the Sword

The cumulative evidence of various NT documents makes it clear that Jesus repudiated the use of the sword for advancing the kingdom of God, as did his followers. However, Luke 22:35-38 is sometimes cited to suggest otherwise because of the way the word "sword" is used. In this passage, Jesus is speaking to the disciples shortly before his arrest:

> And he said to them, "When I sent you out with no moneybag or knapsack or sandals, did you lack anything?" They said, "Nothing." He said to them, "But now let the one who has a moneybag take it, and likewise a knapsack. And let the one who has no sword sell his cloak and buy one. For I tell you that this Scripture must be fulfilled in me: 'And he was numbered with the transgressors.' For what is written about me has its fulfillment." And they said, "Look, Lord, here are two swords." And he said to them, "It is enough."[11]

This passage has been widely debated because of its brief and seemingly cryptic message about buying a sword. Even within the wider context of Luke's account it is stated that Jesus stopped the use of the sword by a disciple and healed the servant whose ear had been cut off (Luke 22:49-51). Jesus then questions why the crowd had come out against him with swords and clubs (Luke 22:52), indicating the non-violent nature of his mission. So even within Luke's context it is clear that Jesus is not a revolutionary who is advocating the use of the sword to advance his cause.

Regarding the reference to buying a sword in Luke 22:36, there have been various interpretations. John Calvin (d. 1564) and John Wesley (d. 1791) both interpreted this reference to the sword in a symbolic sense. Calvin identifies the passage as using metaphorical language,[12] and states that "he does not call them to an outward conflict, but only, under the comparison of fighting, he warns them of the severe struggles of temptations which they must undergo, and

---

11. Luke 22:35-38.
12. Calvin, *Matthew, Mark and Luke*, 136-37.

CHANGES REGARDING THE USE OF THE SWORD

of the fierce attacks which they must sustain in spiritual contests."[13] Wesley briefly comments on Luke 22:36: "He that hath no sword, let him sell his garment and buy one—It is plain, this is not to be taken literally. It only means, this will be a time of extreme danger."[14]

Craig Keener identifies the passage in Luke 22 as containing a real but symbolic act to fulfill the prophetic passage in Isaiah 53:12:

> By mentioning the "sword" here Jesus is not inviting revolution like the *zealots did (cf. *Pseudo-Phocylides 32–34). Instead, Jesus calls for a temporary and symbolic act—two are sufficient (v. 38)—so he may be charged as a revolutionary and hence "reckoned among transgressors" in accordance with Isaiah 53:12.[15]

It is clear in Luke 22:37 that Jesus is said to be citing Isaiah 53:12 as being directly fulfilled in his own person in the events that would follow. He would be reckoned among transgressors as a result of his arrest, trial, and crucifixion. The swords have been seen as the reason why Christ was numbered among the transgressors.[16] What would be debated is whether it is the swords themselves that fulfill Christ being numbered among transgressors, or if it is the earlier instructions of Christ to his disciples (Luke 22:35–36) that are given to them because he would soon be numbered among the transgressors.

Others have taken the approach that the instruction to buy a sword was an acknowledgement that the disciples would be thrust into new dangers and would need the sword as protection against wild animals and robbers in their travels."[17] In this approach, the use of the sword is seen as being for defensive purposes only because of Jesus' reference to being sent out on the mission to spread the gospel and traveling to various places (Luke 22:35–36). This slant has been taken in some older commentaries and has been promoted by more recent interpretations as well.[18] This approach is

---

13. Calvin, *Matthew, Mark and Luke*, 136.
14. Wesley, *Explanatory Notes*, Luke 22:36.
15. Keener, *Bible Background Commentary*, 250.
16. Martin, "Luke," 260.
17. Gundry, *New Testament*, 332–33.
18. Kattathara, "Snag of the Sword," 172–74.

certainly more plausible than the idea that Jesus was wavering in his commitment to a non-violent surrender to the cross, or that Jesus was "trying to discern the will of the Father through the lens of the biblical strands of holy war and the Suffering Servant."[19] Perhaps it would be better to admit that "likely there are no completely satisfying answers to the puzzle of the so-called two swords passage."[20]

Occasionally more recent scholars have taken the position that the reference to the sword in Luke 22 is evidence that Jesus was really a proto-zealot who was advocating rebellion against Rome, but that most evidence of this was suppressed by the NT writings in order to curry the favor of the Roman Empire. The idea that "Jesus led his followers, armed, to Jerusalem to participate in a heavenly-earthly battle to overthrow the Romans and their high-priestly client rulers of Judea."[21] fails for a lack of supporting evidence from the NT sources or evidence from early church history. It is widely attested that early Christianity was to a large extent pacifistic.[22] How a precursor of the Zealots (or any advocate of armed rebellion) could give rise to this non-violent movement has never been sufficiently demonstrated. The context and background of Luke 22 indicates that the passage cannot be understood "in a Zealot-like manner."[23]

Summary of Luke 22

Within the context of Luke 22 itself, Jesus clearly renounces the use of the sword to prevent his arrest (Luke 22:49–51). This repudiation of the use of violent means to defend himself or his cause is also confirmed in other NT passages (Matt 26:50–56; John 18:34–38). Acts also clearly indicates that the disciples fled from persecution rather than resorting to the sword (Acts 8:1–4; 13:50–51; 14:2–20; 17:1–14; 20:1–3). So whatever else the passage in Luke means, it cannot be used to support the idea that Jesus (or his followers)

19. Schertz, "Swords and Prayer," 122.
20. Schertz, "Swords and Prayer," 120.
21. Martin, "Armed and Not Dangerous," 3.
22. cf. Latourette, *History of Christianity*, 242–43.
23. Kattathara, "Snag of the Sword," 170.

justified the use of the sword to advance the kingdom of God, spread Christianity, or resist persecution.

Was Jesus speaking symbolically about buying a sword, or was it a literal statement? This seems to be the crux of the debate. There is a suggestion of plausibility about the use of the sword for self-defense from wild animals and robbers because of the challenging situations the disciples would find themselves in. However, this would be the only passage in the NT that could be cited to support this position, making it tenuous. In the symbolic vs literal debate, there are other examples where Jesus spoke symbolically but was taken literally (cf. Mark 8:14–21; John 2:13–22). The passage in Luke 22 reveals confusion among the disciples about what Jesus meant in reference to the sword—and later in the passage Jesus clearly renounces the use of the sword to prevent his arrest. This lends more support to the idea that Jesus was speaking symbolically about the sword (as he did elsewhere—cf. Matt 10:34–37).

The number of diverse interpretations of this passage are a reminder that this is a cryptic statement of Jesus—a statement that to this day is widely debated as to its intended meaning and has given rise to a number of different interpretations. However, the wider context in Luke and the rest of the NT is clear in ruling out Jesus as an armed revolutionary. Luke clearly demonstrates that Jesus renounced the use of the sword to prevent his arrest.

The debate about the Luke 22 passage does not alter the basic conclusion in this study about the use of the sword in the NT: Jesus led a non-violent movement; he repudiated the use of the sword to advance the kingdom of God, to prevent his arrest, or to spread Christianity. The early church followed his example and did not use the sword to advance Christianity or to resist persecution. They fled persecution rather than engaging in violent resistance.

So the freely gathered communities of faith outlined in the NT provide a sharp contrast with the OT nation of Israel and its use of the sword as illustrated previously. While the OT nation of Israel had been given the divinely authorized use of the sword, the NT apostles were told by their founder, "Put your sword back into its place. For all who take the sword will perish by the sword" (Matt 26:52). Since the kingdom of Jesus was not of this world, his band of followers would not engage in an armed conflict (John 18:36). Whatever other political implications may be gleaned from the teaching of Jesus, it does not include armed violence in the name of Christ.

Paul and the Sword

While Jesus forbade his disciples from "taking up the sword" to advance Christianity, some years later, Paul speaks of another group of people who are "given" the sword: national governments. The key passage is Romans 13:1–7. Speaking of national rulers in verses 3–4, Paul describes them bearing the sword as servants of God, saying,

> for rulers are not a terror to good conduct, but to bad. Would you have no fear of the one who is in authority? Then do what is good, and you will receive his approval, for he is God's servant for your good. But if you do wrong, be afraid, for he does not bear the sword in vain. For he is the servant of God, an avenger who carries out God's wrath on the wrongdoer.[24]

Romans 13:1–7 is a key passage regarding the role of human governments and the way that Christ's followers should relate to governments. This passage serves as a watershed when seen in the larger context of the OT and NT people of God. In the OT background, the nation of Israel had the use of the sword to ensure the nation's survival in the midst of evil in the world. In the NT, Gentile governments are shown to have a God-given use of the sword to restrain and punish evildoers in society (Rom 13:3–4). In contrast, the NT church is given no divine mandate for using the sword either in Paul's writings or elsewhere in the NT.

Paul is widely acknowledged as the author of Romans. The approximate time of writing has also been well established by comparing data in Acts and Paul's other writings with information in Romans. It is estimated that Paul wrote Romans in AD 56 or 57 in the earlier part of Nero's reign.[25] The historical setting of the believers in Rome will provide significant insights in regard to Romans 13:1–7.

24. Rom 13:3–4.
25. Witherington, *New Testament History*, 5633.

Changes Regarding the Use of the Sword

The Sword and Lethal Punishment in Paul's OT Background

Romans 13:1–7 has some significant implications when considering Paul's interpretive matrix in the OT writings. In Israel's OT history, the use of lethal force was given religious sanction for both external military threats and internal threats to the holiness and well-being of the nation because of things such as idolatry, sexual perversion, and murder (Exod 22:19–20; 21:12). Clearly, the OT perspective is that the nation of Israel was given the use of lethal force for internal and external threats. However, there was also the understanding that when Israel became enmeshed in idolatry and violated the covenant, God's protection of the nation could be lifted and Israel could be defeated by its enemies (Amos 7:9–17; Jer 19:7; 32:24–28). In the OT, there is a punitive reason that Gentile nations are able to use the sword successfully against Israel. In contrast, Romans 13:1–7 outlines a different use of the sword by Gentile governments: to restrain evildoers within the Gentile nations.

Religious Violence, Paul's Conversion, and Non-Resistance

It is helpful at this point to consider Paul's pre-conversion beliefs concerning the use of lethal force by Israel's religious leaders. As a Pharisee, Paul was extremely zealous for the Law (Gal 1:14). The Pharisees of this time period were not happy with the Roman occupation. Some Pharisees passively accepted the Roman occupation as a divine punishment, while others advocated the use of the sword to redeem Israel.[26] Regardless of which group Paul was in, as a zealous Pharisee he still advocated that the Jewish religious leaders could use lethal force if needed as part of their religious authority over the Jewish people. This is seen in statements in Paul's letters and his pre-conversion actions (Acts 9:1–2; 26:10; Gal 1:13).

Paul acknowledged that, prior to his conversion, he violently persecuted the Christians (1 Tim 1:13). He persecuted the church and tried to destroy it (Gal 1:13). The author of Acts recounts Paul's testimony, that he "persecuted this Way to the death, binding and

---

26. Barnett, *Early Christianity*, 139.

delivering to prison both men and women" (Acts 22:4). Standing before Agrippa, Paul's testimony described in Acts is that he not only locked up many of the believers in prison after receiving authority from the chief priests, but when they were put to death, he cast his vote against them (Acts 26:10). Paul was present at the stoning of Stephen and was in agreement with putting him to death (Acts 8:1). Keener notes that the Romans did not allow their subjects to execute people, but Stephen's hearers became enraged and killed him based on Jewish law.[27] Paul was in agreement with this lethal use of force.

Clearly, prior to his conversion, Paul supported the use of lethal force as a tool of Israel's religious leaders to combat the sect of the Nazarenes. This may have had support in Paul's theology (of that time period) from the OT authorization to use lethal force against false prophets (Deut 13:1–5) since he would have considered Jesus a false messiah. Caution would have to be used to avoid antagonizing the Roman authorities since Rome did not allow subject nations to utilize the death penalty.[28] Utilizing the death penalty would have to be done through the Roman authorities or as a covert activity. One exception that seems to have been allowed was the Jewish requirement of the death penalty for any Gentile who trespassed the sanctity of the temple.[29]

Paul's Understanding of the Gospel

Paul's conversion on the road to Damascus unleashed a dramatic revolution in his life and his thinking. Paul went from being a persecutor of the church to a leading proponent of Jesus as the Messiah. Although the full implications would only become apparent over a longer period of time, the revelation that Jesus was the crucified and risen Messiah completely re-set the direction of Paul's thinking. This would change his views on the religious use of lethal force. Key issues for consideration here regarding Paul's NT

27. Keener, *Bible Background Commentary*, 342.
28. Keener, *Bible Background Commentary*, 342.
29. Witherington, *New Testament History*, 2833–39.

viewpoint are the facts that (1) he came to understand that Christ's followers would be composed of Jews and Gentiles as the body of Christ (Eph 2:11–22; 3:4–6; Rom 15:8–18; 1 Cor 1:22–24); (2) the body of Christ would be made up of freely gathered followers of Christ, the ecclesia, gathered in the various nations where the gospel would be preached (1 Cor 1:2; Rom 1:1–5; 15:15–21); (3) national governments are seen as having the use of the sword to punish evildoers (Rom 13:1–7). Paul shows no evidence of advocating violence by the church either in religious matters or in response to the Roman government. Paul counsels the Roman believers that they should not avenge themselves (Rom 12:17–21), and that they should submit to the government (Rom 13:1, 5). While Paul advocated the use of excommunication to deal with a persistent sinner (1 Cor 5:9–13), there is no evidence that he gave religious sanction to the use of the sword to deal with internal threats to the Christian community or external persecution.

The messianic rule of Jesus was not an earthly political rule in Paul's writings, and the kingdom of God was not a physical kingdom of this world (Rom 14:17; 1 Cor 15:50). In this, Paul clearly follows the foundation laid by Jesus and kept by the original apostles. Jewish expectations of a political Messiah who would rule the nations, however varied those messianic expectations might have been, were sorely disappointed in Jesus. Paul emphasized a heavenly Messiah and future resurrection, saying, "But our citizenship is in heaven, and from it we await a Savior, the Lord Jesus Christ, who will transform our lowly body to be like his glorious body, by the power that enables him even to subject all things to himself" (Phil 3:20–21).

The Influence of Jesus

Paul would have seen firsthand the attitude of Stephen towards his persecutors as Stephen knelt and prayed that the Lord would forgive them (Acts 7:60). This would have traced back to the example of Jesus himself in how he forgave those who sent him to the cross (Luke 23:34; cf. 6:35–37). Through his contacts with the other apostles and other early believers, Paul would undoubtedly have become aware of how Jesus repudiated the use of the sword. The way Jesus responded to the religious authorities and to Pilate would have been widely known among His followers.

Paul fully adopted the non-violent approach of Jesus as can be seen in the book of Acts and in Paul's writings. Paul now flees from persecutions rather than starting persecutions. This provides a sharp contrast with his previous authorization of violence against the Christians. The realization that he had been wrong to persecute the Christians and had contributed to their imprisonment and in some cases wrongful deaths had a profound and long lasting impact on Paul, as is well documented in his writings years later (1 Cor 15:8-10; Gal 1:13-23). Paul's own endurance of persecution is noteworthy. Paul flees from persecution rather than mounting any sort of armed resistance (Acts 14:1-7; 2 Cor 11:23-33; 2 Tim 3:10-11). All of this provides background for Romans 13:1-7 and Paul's understanding of the use of the sword. While governments have been given the use of the sword, the same cannot be said for the church.

The Literary Context: Romans 12:17-21

The immediate literary context of Romans 13:1-7 is significant. Immediately before the Romans 13:1-7 passage, Paul tells the Roman believer,

> Repay no one evil for evil, but give thought to do what is honorable in the sight of all. If possible, so far as it depends on you, live peaceably with all. Beloved, never avenge yourselves, but leave it to the wrath of God, for it is written, "Vengeance is mine, I will repay, says the Lord." To the contrary, "if your enemy is hungry, feed him; if he is thirsty, give him something to drink; for by so doing you will heap burning coals on his head." Do not be overcome by evil, but overcome evil with good.[30]

Paul's counsel is to never repay evil for evil (Rom 12:17). The believers in Rome should never avenge themselves. Instead, they should

---

30. Rom 12:17-21.

leave this to God's wrath (Rom 12:19). This would have both personal and public applications. The public application is particularly seen in Paul's statement that the believers in Rome should "give thought to what is honorable in the sight of all" (Rom 12:17). There would have been real temptations to rebel against authority as a response to persecution. Paul had personally experienced persecution from both religious leaders and political leaders. These would have been situations where Paul would have faced the temptation to avenge himself. Romans 12:17–21 has clear links to Romans 13:1–7 because resisting authorities (Rom 13:2) would have been a familiar form of taking vengeance against one's enemies in the public arena in Paul's time. There were definite temptations for agitation against Rome, and there is evidence of such agitations in Rome during this time period.[31]

Within a few years of the writing of Romans, the Zealot-sponsored uprising against the Roman authorities would cost the Jewish people their nation. Tumults and riots had occurred even in the Roman capital, and Paul is advising the Roman believers to maintain a good public example as a way of doing what is honorable in the sight of all (Rom 12:17). Advice to honor those in authority and obey the laws was common in ancient authors of the time and was "incorporated into the Christian culture as well" in passages such as Romans 13:7 and 1 Peter 2:17, according to David deSilva.[32] Honoring those in positions of authority was a significant ideal in Greco-Roman society.[33]

Romans 13:1–7 in its Historical and Cultural Context

"Let every person be subject to the governing authorities" (Rom 13:1) is Paul's general counsel to the believers in Rome in regard to their attitude towards governmental authority. Paul is concerned that Christ's followers have a responsible and good attitude towards the government so as not to discredit their witness in the Greco-Roman culture.

---

31. Moo, "Romans," 1152.

32. deSilva, *Honor, Patronage, Kinship and Purity*, 83.

33. deSilva, *Honor, Patronage, Kinship and Purity*, 83.

Paul establishes that "there is no authority except from God, and those that exist have been instituted by God" (Rom 13:1). This should be taken to mean that just as God established the boundaries of nations (Acts 17:26), he has also established the governmental authority structures for those nations. Although God has established those authority structures, Paul is describing how governmental authority should function in society without addressing situations where it fails to fulfill its legitimate role or becomes oppressive by contravening God's higher authority.[34] Those who resist the authorities will bring judgment on themselves (Rom 13:2). When Paul says that "rulers are not a terror to good conduct, but to bad" (Rom 13:3) he is describing the normal function of government without addressing possible exceptions.[35]

The statement that the authorities bear the sword and are servants of God (Rom 13:4) highlights the development of Paul's thought in relation to non-Jewish governments. These governments, rather than being completely evil or completely separated from God, have God-given functions and responsibilities. Paul, writing as an apostle to the Gentiles and writing to believers in Rome, develops a concept of non-Jewish government here that provides additional detail beyond what Jesus or Old Testament teachings had explicitly addressed[36]. As Paul develops this teaching, governments bear the sword in order to restrain evil and to punish evildoers and government leaders are considered to be servants of God. The believer was not to rebel against government authority. Believers are to pay taxes to avoid being seen as rebellious towards the Roman government and to support the government in its God-given roles (Rom 13:5-7).

---

34. Moo, "Romans," 1153.

35. Keener, *Romans*, 154.

36. There are OT examples of God using Gentile rulers (2 Chron 36:23; Isa 45:1-4) and Jewish people having a submissive attitude towards them at times; but the explicit teaching that God gives the sword to Gentile rulers to restrain evil within their nations was more fully developed in Romans 13:1-7.

CHANGES REGARDING THE USE OF THE SWORD

The Wider New Testament Context of Submission

The wider NT context must also be taken into consideration in relation to Romans 13. Paul cannot be expected to address issues regarding submission to totalitarian governments that would exist in the twentieth or twenty-first century.[37] Yet in the wider context of the NT, a situation did arise where submission to a higher authority came into play. When Peter and the other apostles were ordered to stop preaching in the name of Jesus, their answer was "whether it is right in the sight of God to listen to you rather than to God, you must judge, for we cannot but speak of what we have seen and heard" (Acts 4:19-20). When ordered to stop preaching, submission to a higher authority than the government or religious authorities came into play, involving submission to God. There is no evidence that the early apostles resisted the religious or political authorities in Jerusalem through violent means. Rather than resisting these authorities with the sword, the apostles viewed themselves as submitting to a higher authority from God because they were commanded to preach the gospel. In doing this, they continued to follow the non-violent approach taught and exemplified by Jesus (Matt 26:50-54; 5:43-48; John 18:33-38).

Conclusions Regarding Romans 13:1-7

Romans 13:1-7 marks a new expression of Pauline thought which was stated in response to the situation of Christ's followers in Rome at the time of writing. The normal function of government is presented without considering possible exceptions.[38] Human governments are required to use their authority, including lethal force, to stop wrongdoers from inflicting harm on society. Although Yoder rightly objects to just war theory advocates using Romans 13 to suggest that believers have a duty to be involved in military or police action[39] he wants to deny the God-given aspect of the sword for

---

37. Keener, *Romans*, 155-56.
38. Moo, "Romans," 1153.
39. Yoder, *Politics of Jesus*, 193-94.

human government and instead suggests it is an accommodation to evil.[40] In Romans 13:1–4, governmental authority is shown to have a God-given role rather than simply being an accommodation to evil. Believers are counseled to submit to the authority of the government in part to avoid being identified as a group that is subversive to Rome, and in part as a demonstration of a conscience that is clear of wrongdoing (Rom 13:5).

In the wider literary context of the OT and NT writings, Romans 13:1–7 marks a watershed. In the OT nation of Israel, God's people are given divine sanction for using the sword to ensure the survival of the nation. In the NT, particularly as the concept is developed in Romans 13:1–7, the Gentile national governments have been given the use of the sword in order to restrain and punish wrongdoers. In contrast, the NT church as described in Paul's writings and elsewhere in the NT does not have the use of the sword. Paul never advises armed resistance against enemies in any of his writings to the NT churches.

All of the evidence points to the fact that the NT church no longer has the divine sanction for using the sword that existed in the OT. The church cannot use the sword to advance Christianity; the church cannot use the sword to respond to persecution; and the church cannot use the sword to deal with internal threats to its holiness. Excommunication is the only option for dealing with one who persistently practices sin since the church consists of freely gathered communities in various parts of the Roman Empire. The communities were formed through the spread of the gospel; government authorities had the use of force in those locales, not the church.

Instead of a blind defense of the status quo of national governments, Romans 13:1–7 is more accurately seen as a radical departure for the people of God. No longer given divine sanction for the use of the sword as they were in the OT, the believers in Rome are to submit to the authorities within their sphere of governance. Paul does not address situations where the government directly usurps God's own authority over his people; the religious, political, historical, and social background of Romans 13:1–7 show that Paul's

---

40. Yoder, *Politics of Jesus*, 198.

counsel to the believers in Rome was understandably to cooperate with government as good subjects and citizens of Rome. This was necessary to avoid being viewed as subversive.

What Paul does not address in Romans 13:1–7 is understandable because he was writing in a particular context to a particular group of people in Rome during the more peaceful portion of Nero's reign. Paul does not address whether or not Christ's followers should serve in the government or the military; nor does he address the emperor cult developments that would take place in the Roman Empire where believers would be forced to choose between worshipping the emperor or being killed.[41]

What is seen in the earlier context of Romans as well as the book of Acts is that Paul adopted the non-violent approach of Jesus rather than advocating the use of the sword by Christ's followers to resist persecution or advance the gospel. The historical importance of this dimension of Christianity can hardly be overstated. The principles of Romans 13:1–7 follow closely upon Paul's earlier statements not to avenge oneself or take revenge, while continuing the commitment of the church to not pick up the sword.

The Sword Transformed

The symbol of the sword and other weaponry is also transformed in Paul's writings. Since Christ's followers are not called to conquer physical lands through the use of the sword, the natural corollary to the transformed symbol regarding land in Paul is a transformation regarding battle imagery. As Paul states it, "though we walk in the flesh, we are not waging war according to the flesh. For the weapons of our warfare are not of the flesh but have divine power to destroy strongholds. We destroy arguments and every lofty opinion raised against the knowledge of God, and take every thought captive to obey Christ" (2 Cor 10: 3–5). The armor and weaponry of the believer is spiritual in nature (Eph 6:13–18; Rom 13:12; 1 Thess 5:8). The battle shifts from "an *ethnic* to a *cosmic* battle."[42] This

---

41. Keener, *Romans*, 154.
42. Wright, *Paul and the Faithfulness of God*, 11141.

should be seen as a shift from the battle of the Abrahamic people of God in relation to their Promised Land to the battle for the souls of humankind in relation to the gospel of Christ. Paul sees himself involved in a great battle —not against human or physical enemies, but against "sin and death themselves."[43]

Wider New Testament Considerations

It is clear that, in his teaching and example, Jesus forbade his followers from using the sword to advance God's kingdom or resist persecutors, and this teaching was continued in the early church.[44] In Matthew's Gospel, when Jesus tells Peter immediately before his arrest, "Put your sword back into its place. For all who take the sword will perish by the sword" (Matt 26:52; cf. John 18:10), this statement is given as a clear principle for Christ's followers that they were not to take up the sword to advance the kingdom of God. In Acts, there is no record of Christ's followers arming themselves in order to resist persecution. Their one recourse was to flee, and that is what they did at various times (Acts 8:1-4; 13:50-51; 14:2-20; 20:1-3; 17:1-14; cf. Matt 10:23). Fleeing is not an argument from silence regarding early Christians using the sword in relation to Christianity; it is an argument that is based on Christian praxis. Since divine land promises were not part of the new agenda for the church, and the freely gathered communities of faith were to exist in every nation, they were not given the sword to protect or obtain a Promised Land. They fled to escape persecution and this was a key factor in spreading the gospel.

While it is clear that Jesus forbade his followers from using the sword to advance God's kingdom or to resist persecution, there are some unanswered questions in the NT regarding the use of lethal force. In Romans 13:1-7, Paul addresses the need for a submissive attitude by believers to governmental authority and makes it clear

---

43. Wright, *Paul and the Faithfulness of God*, 11096-99.

44. Particularly significant passages include John 18:33-37; Luke 6:27-29; 22:47-51; 23:32-34; Matt 26:47-52; 10:23; 1 Pet 2:19-23; Rom 12:18-21; 8:35-39; Acts 8:1-4; 13:50-51; 14:2-7; 14:19-20; 17:1-14; 20:1-3.

that government leaders have been given the use of force to stop evildoers (13:4). But in Romans 13 or elsewhere, Paul does not directly address whether or not followers of Christ should have a role in governments. Paul never addresses whether or not believers would be allowed to utilize the sword as part of a role in a human government. This question was apparently not pressing at the time and was not addressed by Paul in Romans 13:1–7.

In Romans 13, governmental authorities have been given the use of lethal force as servants of God to stop those who do evil (Rom 13:4). Therefore, while Jesus forbids his followers to take up the sword in order to advance the gospel or to resist persecution (Matt 26:51–52), governmental authorities have been "given" the sword to use against evildoers. So if Christians participate in government, can they thereby be "given" the use of the sword as members of the police force or military, or does the prohibition against "taking up the sword" apply to Christ's followers across the board? Pacifists in church history have held to the latter, while other Christian traditions have held that Christ's followers can participate in the governmental use of the sword described in Romans 13. The massive and centuries-old debate on these two positions cannot be pursued here.

Obviously, the "crusade" justification for war used by the church in the Middle Ages cannot claim any justification from the NT because the example and teaching of Jesus and the early church clearly forbid the church from pursuing any such action. For the NT church, the focus had clearly shifted away from land promises and any reliance on the physical sword to a spiritual battle with spiritual armor and the sword of the Spirit which is the word of God (Eph 6:13–17).

Summary on the Use of the Sword

In regard to the use of the sword, the thesis provides a clear explanation. This major discontinuity between the OT and the NT can be best explained as the difference between God's instructions for a nation in the OT, and God's instructions in the NT for freely gathered communities of faith in Christ that would exist throughout the nations. Governmental authorities in various nations have use of the sword for the purpose of restraining evil and protecting their people, but the NT communities would not be given the use of the sword to advance Christianity, punish evildoers, or resist persecution.

In the OT, the use of the sword was given to a nation in connection with its land and its societal laws; NT communities of faith are different. The nation of Israel had a Promised Land, and although some of the NT communities of faith existed within Israel, they never had the governance of the nation. As the church expanded into the Greco-Roman world, they did so without taking new lands. Since the new communities were composed of Jewish and Gentile followers of Christ who had freely gathered, they were a different social structure than a nation. They were a faith community, the new temple made up of living stones who were built upon the foundation of Christ (Eph 2:11–22). Since the destination of the church was to make disciples within every nations, the land promises of the OT were set aside to fulfill the new vision.

Although there is significant discontinuity because of these changes, there are also major areas of continuity between the OT and NT. This is important to note for the sake of balance. For Paul, the OT writings are the Scriptures that were "written for our instruction" (Rom 15:4). The Messiah that is foretold in God's messages to Israel is fulfilled in the person of Jesus. There are many areas of continuity as OT teachings regarding God, as well as human relationships, are repeated or enlarged upon in the NT. The NT vision does not mean that God has abandoned Israel; in Romans 9–11, Paul makes it clear that God has not rejected his people (cf. Rom 11:1). There is still a future for Israel in God's plans (Rom 11:11–31). The new communities would invite Jews and Gentiles to follow Christ and become part of the living temple that he was building (1 Cor 3:11–17). These communities were to be formed upon the foundation of Christ in all nations and, therefore, could not be established on divine land promises or the use of the sword. There was only one theocratic nation. While there are many examples of moral and spiritual teaching that continue from the OT into the NT, the use of the sword, stoning, and other human means of inflicting physical punishment are notably absent.

6

Changes Regarding the Temple

The Temple of Israel

Along with land and sword, the OT symbol of the temple also undergoes major transformation in the NT. What is striking is the massive amount of change this involves. Ultimately, the sacrificial system of the temple is no longer deemed necessary, and the freely gathered communities of faith in Christ *become* the new temple of God. This also means that the OT laws concerning the priesthood and the numerous sacrificial regulations are set aside as requirements for the body of Christ. Key points concerning the temple must be analyzed and related to their transformed emphasis in the NT.

The Jerusalem temple traced its beginnings to the moveable tabernacle established in the wilderness (Exod 26—27). Prior to the monarchy, the portable tabernacle was established first at Shiloh, and later at Gibeon (Josh 18:1; 1 Chron 21:19). The tabernacle was eventually brought to Jerusalem by David, and he made the preparations for Solomon to build a permanent temple in Jerusalem for Yahweh (2 Sam 6:12–19; 1 Chron. 28:1–21). The tabernacle and later the temple became the vital focus of Jewish religious life, centering on the sacrificial system, the priesthood, and the presence of God. The emphasis on the presence of God in the Holy of

Holies, as well as the priesthood and the sacrificial system taught in the Pentateuch, meant that the tabernacle/temple would be a major focus in Jewish history.

Exile and Return: The Centrality of the Temple

The destruction of the city of Jerusalem and the temple by the Babylonians was a crushing blow to the Jewish nation. Jeremiah had warned against the false security of trusting in the invincibility of the temple (Jer 7:3–15). Instead, he called the people to forsake injustice, idolatry, and other sins so that destruction would not overtake them (Jer 7:5–7). But when the temple was destroyed in 587–586 BC, "it then became the object of hope for future restoration."[1]

The return from exile was a time of rebuilding, and Israel was assisted at this time by Gentile rulers. "The return from the exile was both a return to the city and to rebuild the temple; the temple became the center of both the religious and political life of the post-exilic community."[2] The rebuilding of the temple restored the ability to offer sacrifices as prescribed by the Torah. This rebuilt temple provided a central focus for Jewish religious life in the centuries leading up to the NT era.

The temple in Jerusalem was still a major focus of the Jewish people at the time of Christ: "At the heart of Jewish national life, for better or worse, stood the Temple. All around, looking to the Temple as its center, lay the Land which the covenant God had promised to give to Israel, which was thus his by right and hers by promise."[3] The temple was the place where the priests and Levites fulfilled their various duties regarding the sacrificial offerings. The Torah included detailed instructions regarding the duties of priests, offerings, and regulations concerning holy space. More than just a symbolic edifice, the temple was "the place where YHWH lived and ruled in the midst of Israel."[4]

1. Noll, "Tabernacle, Temple," 1166.
2. Davies, *Gospel and the Land*, 152.
3. Wright, *People of God*, 224.
4. Wright, *People of God*, 224.

The Temple and God's Presence

The tabernacle and later the Jerusalem temple are "the most prominent way God's presence is experienced in the Old Testament."[5] The Pentateuch includes the emphasis that the tabernacle was to be a sanctuary so that Yahweh would dwell in their midst (Exod 25:8). This would fulfill the purpose of God, who brought the Israelites out of Egypt that He might dwell among them and be their God (Exod 29:45–46). In the Holy Place inside the veil, Yahweh would appear in a cloud over the mercy seat (Lev 16:2). The association of the tabernacle with the presence of God was a key feature of early Israelite religion.

This focus on the presence of God continued in the monarchy. At the dedication of the permanent temple in Jerusalem, the glory of the Lord filled the temple in a cloud (1 Kgs 8:10–13), signifying that the presence of the Lord was there. At the time of dedication, Solomon acknowledged the temple as the place where God's presence would indeed dwell (1 Kgs 8:13) but also confessed that heaven and the highest heaven could not contain God's presence, much less the house that he had built (1 Kgs 8:27). So, while the temple was acknowledged as the place of God's presence, belief in the greatness and transcendence of God was also expressed. This belief in the transcendence of God's presence was also expressed in prophetic passages such as Isaiah 66:1–2, and the prophet Jeremiah warned against trusting in the temple as a guarantee of God's presence while there was oppression, injustice, immorality, and idolatry among God's people (Jer 7:3–15). So, while the temple is the special focus of God's presence in the OT, it does not provide an absolute guarantee that God would continue to dwell among His people.

Holiness and God's Presence

God is self-described as being holy (Lev 19:2; 21:8). He intends his holiness to be communicated to his people because of their close association with him. Therefore he says, "You shall be holy, for I the

---

5. Fee, *People of God*, 10.

Lord your God am holy" (Lev19:2). According to Roger Cotton, "the Lord is holy not as one of His qualities but as a summary of all his qualities as the Only God who made the universe and who is separate from all his creation."[6] Only God is holy by nature.[7] "The holiness of anything else is derived, either from God's presence or from consecration to the sanctuary."[8]

By being in covenant with the Lord God, Israel is brought into close relationship with God and therefore shares in his holiness. God necessitated obedience to his covenant instructions and teaching in order to for his holy presence to continue with his people.[9] God's presence would then have a sanctifying effect upon God's people.[10] Close adherence to the rules of the sanctuary and the distinction between clean and unclean are also required, so that God's presence would be honored as the Sovereign of his people.[11] So the requirements of holiness include "ethical and moral obligations as well as cultic and ritual ones."[12] John Hartley summarizes the various aspects of holiness for Israel:

> Israel's being holy meant: (1) they were in a covenant relationship with God; (2) God was present in their midst; (3) they were to promote justice throughout the community by keeping divine instructions; and (4) they were to observe the rules of ritual purity. Observance of both the ceremonial regulations and the moral law was required for the fulfillment of this call to be holy.[13]

Respecting and honoring the presence of God was a key aspect of the rules regarding sacred space in the sanctuary, and reverence for the presence of God is also inculcated by the rules concerning what is clean and unclean. In Leviticus 20, avoiding what is unclean

---

6. Cotton, "Holiness," 97.
7. Cotton, "Holiness," 98.
8. Hartley, "Holy and Holiness," 420.
9. Cothey, "Ethics and Holiness," 149.
10. Hartley, "Holy and Holiness," 425.
11. Cotton, "Holiness," 98.
12. Cothey, "Ethics and Holiness," 132.
13. Hartley, "Holy and Holiness," 425.

is linked to holiness; Israel is to avoid what is unclean because they are holy to the Lord (Lev 20:24–26). Laws concerning clean and unclean "created object lessons to train God's people in the proper attitude towards the holiness of God and his gift of salvation."[14] Awareness of sin and defilement, the need for forgiveness, and the importance of obedience to God were key features that related to daily life as well as service in the tabernacle.

Felix Chingota notes that "holiness is an attribute of Yahweh that must find expression in the actual life of the community. Thus holiness is not some abstract concept but one that can be concretized in relationships."[15] This includes ethical teachings regarding one's relationship with God and relationships between God's people.[16] These ethical teachings would safeguard Israel from the corruption and immorality of the surrounding culture, and in a positive sense help them to reflect God's character.[17]

The Temple and Animal Sacrifices

Along with the focus on God's presence, the central reality of the tabernacle and later the temple was the sacrificial system. Animal sacrifices were offered to provide cleansing from ritual impurity and to atone for sin. "To deal with the covenant people's sins, God gave them a place where they might find atonement and be empowered to live according to the divine will."[18] The tabernacle/temple structure was "the only location where sacrificial atonement could be made."[19] Chilton notes that "sacrifices to the Lord elsewhere are specifically prohibited (Deut 12:13–14), and the complete destruction of the 'places' of all other gods is prescribed (Deut 12:2–3)."[20] There was to be only one way of sacrifice: "They could only approach

---

14. Cotton, "Holiness," 98.
15. Chingota, "Leviticus," 160.
16. Chingota, "Leviticus," 160.
17. Cotton, "Holiness," 89.
18. Hartley, "Holy and Holiness," 430.
19. Greene, "Spirit in the Temple," 719; cf. Deut 12:5–14.
20. Chilton, "Temple, Jewish," 1169.

the Lord, the one God, at the one tabernacle through the one priesthood he established and by means of the one sacrificial system he commanded."[21] Atonement and forgiveness restored the people of God.

The creation of the tabernacle was intimately connected with the establishment of the Mosaic covenant (Exod 19–34) and "the instructions to erect the tabernacle must clearly be understood in terms of the covenant itself."[22] This is clearly seen in the sacrificial system and the priestly functions which were centered in the tabernacle and provided atonement for sin and cleansing from ritual defilement. The Day of Atonement provided a yearly ritual to atone for the sins of God's people, and on that day "the two purification (sin) offerings purged the sanctuary of the accumulated pollution released by all the sins committed during the year; as a result, the sanctuary was empowered to continue to function as the place for the people to meet God."[23] The tabernacle was anointed with oil along with all of its furnishings so that it might become holy (Exod 40:9–11). Various laws of ritual purity were designed to honor God's presence as holy in the tabernacle.

Jerusalem and the Temple

Jerusalem received a unique status as the city of the temple: "The construction of the temple by Solomon transforms the status of Jerusalem as a city. It now becomes in a unique way the city of God. According to Psalms 78:68 and 132:13, the Lord chooses Jerusalem to be his dwelling place."[24] Bruce Waltke highlights some key connections concerning Jerusalem, Mount Zion, and the temple:

> The city is glorious because *I AM* chose Zion/Jerusalem and its temple as his unique earthly residence (Pss 46:6; 87:2). God ordered Abraham to offer Isaac as a sacrifice on Mount Zion (Gen 22:2, 14; 2 Chron 3:1), and here

21. Cotton, "The Tabernacle," 93.
22. Williamson, "Covenant," 151.
23. Hartley, "Day of Atonement," 56.
24. Alexander, *Eden to the New Jerusalem*, 45

CHANGES REGARDING THE TEMPLE

Israel's father received *I AM's* oath to bless him and his descendants. *I AM's* own hands established Zion (Exod. 15:17), and the angel of *I AM* pointed it out as the site for the temple.[25]

Davies stresses the importance of Jerusalem in relation to the land by stating, "the hopes for the land became more and more concentrated in those cherished for that city, which seems to have become the quintessence of the land."[26] Jerusalem and the temple are linked together, and "since the texts dealing with the Temple always implicitly, and usually explicitly, implicate the city, just as Jerusalem became the quintessence of the land, so also the Temple became the quintessence of Jerusalem."[27] The land, the city, and the temple were kept secure because of Israel's covenant relationship with Yahweh. Abandoning the covenant relationship would lead to loss of protection by Yahweh. This would mean judgment and expulsion from the land.[28]

TEMPLE IN THE NEW TESTAMENT

At the time of Christ, the temple was still a central feature of Jewish life, although some Jewish sects had issues with the legitimacy of the temple built by Herod or even rejected the temple altogether.[29] In the early NT church, the temple courts are still a place for Christ's followers to gather (Luke 24:52–53; Acts 2:46–47; 3:1; 5:42). There was not an outright rejection of the Jerusalem temple by the early believers. As time went on, however, Stephen was accused of speaking against Moses and the temple ("this holy place"—Acts 6:13; cf. 6:11–14). Wave Nunnally notes that according to Luke, Stephen's controversy with certain Hellenistic Jewish groups (Acts 6:9) occurred "not from within mainstream Palestinian Judaism, but from

---

25. Waltke, *Old Testament Theology*, 546.
26. Davies, *Gospel and the Land*, 131.
27. Davies, *Gospel and the Land*, 152.
28. Wright, *God's People in God's Land*, 13.
29. Wise, "Temple, Jewish," 1171–73.

among outsiders."[30] While James Dunn claims that it is the issue of the temple rather than the messiahship of Jesus which led to the hostility against Stephen,[31] this seems overstated. While a rumor that Stephen was speaking against the temple would certainly have roused hostility against him, so would the claim that he was speaking against Moses and the Law (Acts 6:11–13).

Stephen's final speech included the emphasis that God's presence was not limited to the temple (Acts 7:48–50). But Nunnally notes that "the purpose of Stephen's speech is to point out the consistent pattern of Jewish behavior throughout history: They have always rejected God's messengers and deliverers."[32] The rejection of Jesus by the Jewish leaders and his crucifixion by the Romans were undoubtedly still graphic realities for the early church.

Rumors that Jesus of Nazareth would "destroy this place" (Acts 6:14) could have been a misinterpretation of Jesus' statement concerning the destruction of the temple of his body described in John chapter 2.[33] This could have been twisted into an anti-temple charge regarding Stephen. Temple, the Law of Moses, the messiahship of Jesus—all these issues seem to be in play in the charges against Stephen. Regardless of the amount of conflict that occurred regarding the temple, the persecution that took place after Stephen's stoning scattered the church, and contact with the Jerusalem temple would have been significantly reduced.

Looking at the wider picture, in the NT writings, the emphasis on the OT temple is superseded by the image of the church as the temple of God (1 Cor 3:16–17; Eph 2:19–22; 1 Pet 2:4–6). In Paul's writing, "the use of temple imagery for the church are (1) the place in the New Covenant where God dwells; (2) the place where God's Spirit is now active; and (3) the holiness and purity that must necessarily characterize God's people, both individually and corporately."[34] Paul told the Corinthians, "what agreement has

30. Nunnally, *Book of Acts*, 151.
31. Dunn, *Parting of the Ways*, 64.
32. Nunnally, *Book of Acts*, 153.
33. Nunnally, *Book of Acts*, 152; John 2:19–22; cf. Matt 26:59–61; Mark 15:29–30.
34. Longenecker, "Paul's Vision," 78–79.

the temple of God with idols? For we are the temple of the living God; as God said, 'I will make my dwelling among them and walk among them, and I will be their God, and they shall be my people'" (2 Cor 6:16). Paul describes the bodies of individual believers as the temple of the Holy Spirit (1 Cor 6:18-20), and he describes the believing community as God's temple indwelt by the Spirit (1 Cor 3:16-17). There is both an individual and a corporate emphasis on Christ's followers as God's temple, along with the corresponding reality of the Spirit's indwelling.

This change from OT temple to NT believers as God's dwelling place is a major area of discontinuity between the OT and NT. The coming of the Holy Spirit at Pentecost (Acts 2:1-4) underscored the new reality that the presence of God was now seen to be dwelling with the Jesus movement.[35] Identifying the new communities as God's temple would have highlighted this understanding of God's presence. As new communities of Christ's followers took root in various cities of the Roman Empire, they were identified in temple imagery as God's dwelling places (1 Cor 3:16-17; 2 Cor 6:16; Eph 2:19-22). The presence of God is not only *with* the followers of Christ; the Spirit is said to dwell in these living temples in such a way that His presence is a reality that would impact the life of the community and how individual believers lived out their lives. They could not jeopardize the unity of the community because it would defile this living temple; they could not continue in sinful practices because it would defile them individually and corporately (1 Cor 3:16-17).

The transformation from a physical temple for the OT nation to the community of faith as the temple in the NT is remarkable. No longer tied to a physical temple, the NT communities of faith could flourish as freely gathered communities throughout the Greco-Roman world. The NT communities of faith became increasingly independent from the Jerusalem temple, and the new temple imagery allowed these communities to lay claim to the presence of God as the indwelling reality that was once restricted to the Jerusalem temple. This meant that wherever NT communities would

---

35. Wright, *How God Became King*, 247.

be gathered, the presence of God would be recognized as dwelling within them and among them. God's instructions in the NT are for freely gathered communities of faith in Christ; the temple imagery is a central aspect of this change of focus from the OT nation that was tied to a physical temple, to the freely gathered communities that would spring up wherever the gospel was preached. Ultimately this would result in the setting aside of numerous temple laws, sacrifices, and OT regulations as requirements for Christ's followers.

Corresponding to this change, Acts presents a gradual shift of emphasis from the temple to households where God's people freely gathered. In Acts 1–8 the scenes shift between the temple and household gatherings; but after Stephen's speech and the persecution which followed, the focus shifts largely to households as the place where Christ's followers gathered.[36] Concerning this shift John Elliot notes that "this transition in venue and focus from temple to household charts for Luke the actual historical and geographical movement of the gospel from its inception in the Holy Land, the Holy City and the Holy Place to its dissemination through the households of the diaspora, 'from Jerusalem, Judaea and Samaria to the ends of the earth' (Acts 1:8)."[37] Early Christianity would largely be a household movement, distinct from the temple in Jerusalem and distinct from the synagogue.[38] Groups of believers met in homes, and those with larger homes would sometimes offer them as meeting places. The "household of God" metaphor is used to describe the church (1 Tim 3:15; 1 Pet 4:17; Eph 2:19; cf. Gal 6:10; Matt 10:25; 2 Tim 2:20–23), and "the positive advantage of the household image as applied to the church is that it develops the notion of care for those who are needy within the congregation."[39] Within the household gatherings of believers, the "gospel of universal salvation is socially embodied in a community of 'brothers and sisters' where repentance, faith, forgiveness, generosity, mercy and justice, familial loyalty and friendship unite the faithful with a God

---

36. Elliot, "Temple versus Household," 216–17.
37. Elliot, "Temple versus Household," 238.
38. Elliot, "Temple versus Household," 217, 238–40.
39. Marshall, "Congregation and Ministry," 114.

of mercy and a Servant-Lord."[40] With the development of Christianity as a small group movement which gathered in households, the imagery of the temple as the body of believers provided a key emphasis for the presence of God to be associated with the people of God rather than a physical temple structure.

The NT Temple as a Symbol of Unity: Removal of Jewish-Gentile Distinctions

A massive change for the NT communities was the appropriation of the temple image for the inclusion of both Jews and Gentiles as the people of God. This was "the startling claim that Gentiles qua Gentiles could now enter this new community and become integral components of the true temple of the God of Israel."[41] One of the clearest descriptions of this change is found in Ephesians 2:11–22, where Paul describes the previous separation of the Gentiles from the commonwealth of Israel (Eph 2:12). Now, through Christ and his death on the cross, the dividing wall of hostility has been broken down (Eph 2:14–16), and the Gentiles are no longer strangers and aliens, but "fellow citizens with the saints and members of the household of God" (Eph 2:19). Because of this, a unified people of God is being built into a holy temple in the Lord (Eph 2:21). Jewish and Gentile believers are being joined together as a dwelling place of the presence of God, through faith in Christ. Keener notes that Paul speaks here "of a new temple, in which Jews and Gentiles together become a holy temple, God's household, the dwelling of the Spirit (Eph 2:19–22)."[42] To accomplish the unity between Jews and Gentiles in the new temple meant that Jewish-Gentile distinctions would be removed as requirements for the church. This would have many ramifications and be difficult to accomplish in practice as Jewish and Gentile followers of Christ fellowshipped together as one body of believers—but it would be absolutely essential for the new movement.

40. Elliot, "Temple versus Household," 239.
41. Wardle, *Temple and Early Christian Identity*, 326.
42. Keener, "One New Temple," 79.

Circumcision

The major turning point officially sanctioning the inclusion of the Gentiles was the Jerusalem Council recounted in Acts 15. This was preceded and prepared for by the incident regarding Cornelius and his household, in which Peter was divinely directed to bring these Gentiles the message of Christ. The Holy Spirit fell upon Cornelius and his household in the middle of Peter's sermon, and God gave clear evidence that they had received the Holy Spirit just as the Christ's followers did in Acts 2 (Acts 10:44–48). The Jerusalem Council approved the inclusion of the Gentiles in the Christian communities without circumcision and recognized the legitimacy of the Gentile followers of Christ as part of the people of God (Acts 15:1–13).[43]

Circumcision was the most obvious barrier to Jewish–Gentile unity in Christ; circumcision hearkens back to the covenant with Abraham that led to the development of the nation of Israel (Gen 17:1–13). Paul goes back in Abraham's life prior to the covenant of circumcision to show that it was when Abraham believed God that his faith was reckoned to him as righteousness (Gen 15:1–6; Gal 3:5–18; Rom 4:1–12). Abraham's faith was prior to the covenant of circumcision and prior to the Sinai covenant, so Paul looks back to that prior faith of Abraham for the ground of acceptance of the Gentiles. Faith is seen as the key for the blessing promised to Abraham to be given to the Gentiles. Faith in Christ (who is identified as Abraham's seed or offspring—Gal 3:16) is what enables Gentiles to receive the blessing of the Spirit in fulfillment of the blessing promised to Abraham that would impact all nations (Gal 3:8–14).

In Romans 2:25–29, Paul makes a distinction between inward and outward circumcision. True circumcision is inward (Rom 2:26–29). Paul emphasizes the work of the Spirit by saying, "a Jew is one inwardly, and circumcision is a matter of the heart, by the Spirit, not by the letter. His praise is not from man but from God" (Rom 2:29). In this connection, N. T. Wright notes that "Paul draws on the much older Jewish discussions about 'circumcision of the heart' to make the point that, if it is the heart that matters, the

---

43. Martens, "People of God," 233.

outward circumcision can be seen as itself indifferent."[44] Paul also focuses on this inner circumcision as one that is accomplished by Christ, linking it to the believer's participation in Christ's death and resurrection (Col 2:11-14).

Food Laws

The OT food laws inculcated separation between the ancient Israelites and the Gentiles. Walter Houston points out this effect by stating that "the restrictions governing the diet of the Jews have since ancient times been among the handful of observances most obviously marking them out as different from others and guarding against their assimilation into other cultures."[45] A key passage highlighting this intended effect is Leviticus chapter 20, in which various warnings are given against following the immoral and idolatrous practices of the surrounding nations (20:1-23), followed by instructions to separate the clean animals from the unclean (20:24-25). The intended effect of all of these commands and instructions is clearly stated as promoting a separation from the surrounding peoples so that the Israelites would be holy to the Lord (Lev 20:26). Even by the time of Peter and Cornelius, this intended effect was still clearly evident (Acts 11:1-3; 4-18).

NT Teaching on Clean and Unclean Foods

The Torah distinctions between clean and unclean foods were ultimately removed as a requirement for the people of God in the NT. In Mark's Gospel, Jesus teaches that what goes into a person does not defile him, but rather what comes out of him (Mark 7:18-19). Craig Keener comments on these words of Jesus by saying,

> If Jesus' words are taken literally, they declare the whole clean/unclean distinction emphasized in the law as of only symbolic value. Because this distinction constituted

---

44. Wright, *Paul and the Faithfulness of God*, 10919-23.
45. Houston, "Foods, Clean and Unclean," 326.

one of the main barriers between Jews and Gentiles (see Rom. 14), Jesus' statement opens the way for racial and cultural reconciliation in table fellowship.[46]

Following the statement of Jesus in Mark 7:18–19, the author of Mark adds the comment, "Thus he declared all foods clean" (Mark 7:19). This is an interpretive commentary based on the teaching of Jesus as it was remembered by the apostles and the early church that would directly relate to the issue of the food laws of the OT. Here Mark's gospel provides a key theological justification for removing the distinctions between clean and unclean foods. Gundry's comment on Mark 7:19 is that "Mark breaks in with the notation that Jesus' statement rescinded Old Testament food laws—all of them. If as the Son of Man Jesus has authority to forgive sins on the earth (Mark 2:10), as God's beloved Son he likewise has authority to rescind an Old Testament law."[47] Ultimately this would mean that food would no longer serve as a barrier between Jewish and Gentile believers.

In Paul's ministry, however, there were still tensions at times between Jewish and Gentile followers of Christ regarding food. The challenge was to have a united fellowship (*koinōnia*) in the Christian communities:

> For Paul, *koinōnia* was no abstraction, for it was expressed in a visible way through regular table fellowship, a practice that Peter and Barnabas had also accepted. *Koinōnia* was associated with the communal meal (cf. Acts 2: 42; 1 Cor 10:16–17). For Jews to eat with gentiles was a major break from the past, as Luke's portrayal of Cornelius (Acts 10:41; 11:3) indicates.[48]

The OT food laws would create barriers between Gentiles and Jews as they had in the past, and this is a central reasons these food laws are seen to be obsolete. United table fellowship between Jewish and Gentile followers of Christ was a key issue: "all those who belong to the Messiah, and are defined by Messiah-faithfulness

---

46. Keener, *Bible Background Commentary*, 153.
47. Gundry, *New Testament*, 166.
48. Thompson, *Community Conformed to Christ*, 188.

Changes Regarding the Temple

and baptism, belong at the same table."⁴⁹ The incident described in Galatians 2 makes it clear that this issue was significant enough for Paul to challenge Peter when he withdrew from table fellowship with the Gentiles. Paul's claim was that "before certain men came from James, he [Peter] was eating with the Gentiles; but when they came he drew back and separated himself, fearing the circumcision party" (Gal 2:12).

In Romans 14, Paul gives considerable counsel designed to help people of "weaker" and "stronger" faith live together in unity. While Jews and Gentiles are not identified by name, and other distinctions may also have been in view by Paul, the passage clearly applies to tensions between Jews and Gentiles in regard to clean and unclean food. Commenting on Romans 14, Keener notes that "for Paul, foods themselves are religiously neutral; that is, one may keep food customs because of upbringing, cultural preference or ethnic attachment, but one who keeps them out of the belief that it is religiously profitable is 'weak in faith' (Rom 14:1)."⁵⁰ While Christ's followers are free to eat or not eat various foods, "Paul does not want stumbling blocks placed before those who continue to keep kosher by others eating non-kosher food in front of them (Rom 14:13–21)."⁵¹

Sabbath

The Jewish Sabbath was another key identity marker based on the Torah. While Jewish followers of Christ could continue to keep the Sabbath as part of their Jewish religious background, it is clear that Paul did not require those in the Christian communities to keep the Saturday Sabbath: "Paul is clear, to start with, that the keeping of holy days, like the eating of food, is a matter of 'indifference': someone who keeps the day, keeps it in honor of the Lord, and someone who does not is equally intending thereby to honor the Lord."⁵² To the Colossians, Paul wrote, "let no one pass judgment on

---

49. Wright, *Paul and the Faithfulness of God*, 10894–96.
50. Keener, *Romans*, 163.
51. Keener, *Romans*, 163.
52. Wright, *Paul and the Faithfulness of God*, 10956–58.

you in questions of food and drink, or with regard to a festival or a new moon or a Sabbath. These are a shadow of the things to come, but the substance belongs to Christ" (2:16-17; cf. Rom 14:5-8). Although not codified as a law, the first day of the week assumed a new prominence in the Christian communities as the day that Christ rose from the dead (cf. Acts 20:7; 1 Cor 16:2; John 20:1).

While Jewish followers of Christ could follow the Sabbath laws, it is clear that the keeping of the Saturday Sabbath was not mandatory for the Christian communities made up of Jews and Gentiles. A clarifying passage is Exodus 31, in which the keeping of the Sabbath is specifically identified as a sign of the covenant between God and the people of Israel (31:16-17). Under the New Covenant, "the Sabbath is no longer the sign of the covenant with the Lord."[53] Circumcision, food laws, and Sabbath laws: the removal of these barriers between Jews and Gentiles was necessary in order for there to be a unified community of faith in Christ, the new temple which was identified with the presence of the Holy Spirit (1 Cor 3:10-16).

Animal Sacrifices and the NT Temple

While the Jerusalem temple was a place for offering animal sacrifices in accordance with the instructions of the Torah, in the NT, it becomes clear that Christ fulfilled the ultimate reality to which the animal sacrifices pointed. The shedding of Jesus' blood "effected the ultimate sacrifice to end all sacrifices–he offered it once and signaled its finality by sitting down at God's right hand, never to offer sacrifice of any sort again (Heb 9:12; 25-28; 10:12-18; cf. 1:3; 8:1; 12:2)."[54] N. T. Wright notes that a striking feature of the praxis of the early Christian communities was that "the Christians offered no animal sacrifices."[55] Some early Jewish Christians may have continued to participate in the sacrificial system at the temple for a period of time, "but no Christians offered animal sacrifice *qua* Christians. Nobody ever thought that the worship of the god

---

53. Cotton, "Understanding the Sabbath," 91.
54. Thielman, *The Law and the New Testament*, 123.
55. Wright, *People of God*, 363.

now made known in Jesus of Nazareth required the blood of calves or lambs. At this point the evidence is clear and unambiguous, and its significance is enormous."[56]

Ultimately, the entire sacrificial system and priestly system of the OT are replaced by the NT emphasis on Christ's sacrificial death on the cross. The author of Hebrews points to Christ's fulfillment of all sacrifices:

> Every priest stands daily at his service, offering repeatedly the same sacrifices, which can never take away sins. But when Christ had offered for all time a single sacrifice for sins, he sat down at the right hand of God, waiting from that time until his enemies should be made a footstool for his feet. For by a single offering he has perfected for all time those who are being sanctified. (Heb 10:11-14)

This sacrificial fulfillment of OT sacrifices through Christ involves major changes between the OT and NT.

Paul illustrates this concept of fulfillment of OT ritual since "in a number of references Paul distinctly associates the death of Christ with the Old Testament ritual and concept of sacrifice."[57] Paul wrote while the temple was still standing but sees Christ as the fulfillment of OT sacrifices. Paul clearly uses the language of sacrifice in referring to Jesus. Redemption is through Christ Jesus (Rom 3:24). It is Jesus "whom God put forward as a propitiation by his blood, to be received by faith" (Rom 3:25). Believers are justified by his blood (Rom 5:9). Christ is also identified as the Passover Lamb that has been sacrificed (1 Cor 5:7), and Paul presents the Lord's Supper as a participation in Christ's body and blood (1 Cor 11:23-27; 10:16).

Peter also claims that Christ "bore our sins in his body on the tree" (1 Pet 2:24) and that Christ suffered for sins—the righteous for the unrighteous (1 Pet 3:18). Believers are redeemed by the blood of Christ, a lamb without blemish (1 Pet 1:18-19).Christ's death on behalf of human sins is a message that is repeated in various NT passages.[58]

---

56. Wright, *People of God*, 363.

57. Ladd, *Theology of the New Testament*, 466; see Rom 3:25; 5:9; 8:3; 1 Cor 5:7; Col 1:20; Eph 1:7; 2:13; cf. Ladd, *Theology of the New Testament*, 466-7.

58. cf. Matt 26:27-28; Rom 4:25; 5:6-10; 1 Cor 15:3; 1 John 2:2

The Presence of God in the OT Temple, Transferred to the NT Communities

The OT tabernacle and later the OT temple in Jerusalem were supremely the place where God's presence was to be found. He dwelt between the cherubim, in the Holy Place (Lev 16:2; Exod 25:22). The tabernacle was a reminder of God's presence in the camp (Exod 25:8). God would live among His people because His presence was in the tabernacle. The holiness rules of the tabernacle were a way to honor and emphasize the sacredness of the presence of God.

The outpouring of the Spirit on the Day of Pentecost demonstrated that "a significant transition takes place as God moves from dwelling within the Jerusalem temple to living with the post-Pentecost followers of Jesus."[59] So the theme of the presence of God is continued in the NT, but the focus is now on the community which has faith in Christ. The presence of God dwells particularly in this new temple community: "The presence of God is the key to tracing the theme of sacred *space* in the OT into the NT, where it is developed in terms of sacred *community*."[60] Regarding the temple symbolism in Paul's writings, Gordon Fee notes that "the local church is God's temple in the community where it is placed; and it is so by the presence of the Spirit alone, by whom God has now revisited his people."[61] The presence of the Holy Spirit within Christ's followers meant that the new communities of faith were a genuine temple rather than just a symbolic gesture to the past.

The Temple Transformation

The physical dependence on the Jerusalem temple is minimized over time. The saying of Jesus, "Destroy this temple and in three days I will raise it up," (John 2:19), pointed away from the Jerusalem temple to the temple of His body (John 2:21). John 2:19-21 "suggests that Jesus' body is the replacement for the Jerusalem temple,

---

59. Alexander, *Paradise to the Promised Land*, 235.
60. Averbeck, "Tabernacle," 826.
61. Fee, *People of God*, 19; cf. 1 Cor 3:16-17.

CHANGES REGARDING THE TEMPLE

whose days are numbered as the special locus for the presence of God."[62] In addition, the phrasing in John that "the Word became flesh and tabernacled among us" (John 1:14) points to Christ as the new dwelling place of God. In the Incarnation, "the concepts of temple and body are united."[63] According to Alexander, "the New Testament draws a close parallel between Jesus and the tabernacle/temple. In Jesus, God is viewed as inhabiting human flesh just as he previously inhabited first the tabernacle and then the temple."[64]

There is not a complete repudiation of the physical temple. Paul still visits the temple and even completes a vow of purification there (Acts 21:26-27). But "the new temple consists of *people*: its foundation is Christ."[65] Burge notes that,

> among the three concentric circles of Jewish theological geography (the Temple —Jerusalem—the land) the Temple stood out. This was the ultimate place of holiness and revelation, the focal point of Jewish affections. And yet Paul is willing to argue that the Christian Church represents a new "Temple of God" (1 Cor 3.16-17; 6.19; 2 Cor 6.16).[66]

Individual believers and the corporate community of believers together become the new temple (2 Cor 6:16; 1 Cor 3:16-17; Eph 2:19-22). The temple (the church) is made up of both Jews and Gentiles (Eph 2:11-22). The OT people of God are the physical descendants of Abraham, with some provisions made for non-Jewish proselytes living among them (Exod 12:48-49). The NT people of God are inclusive of both Jewish and Gentile followers of Jesus as the Messiah in the new institution called the church. Together they shared in the fellowship of the Holy Spirit (2 Cor 13:14). Regarding this change, Fred H. Klooster notes that

> there has been one people of God saved by grace throughout the OT and NT; their organization as church

---

62. Hoskins, *Jesus as Fulfillment*, 116.
63. Alexander, *Eden to the New Jerusalem*, 60.
64. Alexander, *Paradise to the Promised Land*, 235.
65. Chamberlin, "Law of Moses and Christ," 4078.
66. Burge, *Jesus and the Land*, 1460-63.

is a uniquely NT phenomenon instituted by Christ in place of the theocratic temple organization of the Sinaitic Covenant. It is introduced, therefore, to meet the new situation arising from the fulfillment of the Abrahamic Covenant that brings Christ's blessings to all nations.[67]

Jerusalem in the OT was made holy by God dwelling in the temple within the city (2 Chron 6:5-6; Ps 76:1-2). It is called the city of God (Pss 87:1-3; 48:1-2). In the NT, Jesus weeps over Jerusalem because it has not received His message (Luke 19:41-42). Jesus prophesies the destruction of Jerusalem (Luke 19:41-44; 21:20-24). He also prophesies the destruction of the temple in similar fashion (Matt 24:1-2; Luke 21:5-6). Jesus does not present a vision of the rebuilding of the physical temple in His eschatological prophecies in the Gospels. Instead, the restoration of Israel will begin in an unexpected direction with the resurrection of Christ.[68]

These and other NT passages amount to a redefining of the temple:

> The holy space of the Jerusalem temple is redefined as a community of holy persons in the New Testament. In the teachings of Paul and Peter, the church, both corporately and individually, is the temple of God (1 Cor 3:16-17, 6:14-20; 1 Pet 2:4-10). The Spirit of God directly indwells every individual within the totality, so that the Spirit corporately indwells the whole.[69]

Why does the new Jesus movement adopt the temple language and present an alternative vision of the temple of God? While there is more than one facet of this issue, the hard reality of rejection must be considered as a factor. Jesus was rejected as the Messiah by Israel's leaders, and this was a difficult reality for the new movement, complete with persecution. The possibility that the Messiah could suffer was a major issue that was related by Christ's followers to OT passages such as Isaiah 53 and Psalm 22, among others. Another key passage was Psalm 118:22-23, with the statement that

---

67. Klooster, "Biblical Method of Salvation," 3251-53.
68. Burge, *Jesus and the Land*, 1220-23.
69. Waltke, *Old Testament Theology*, 578.

Changes Regarding the Temple

"the stone that the builders rejected has become the cornerstone. This is the LORD's doing; it is marvelous in our eyes." In each of the Synoptic Gospels, this passage from Psalm 118 is quoted at the end of the parable of the vineyard told by Jesus in reference to the son being killed as the heir and the vineyard then being given to others (Luke 20:9–19; cf. Matt 21:33–45; Mark 12:1–11). The stone being rejected provides a significant explanation from the Psalms for the rejection of Christ by the Jewish leaders. Jesus "is the messianic stone which, rejected by the builders, takes the chief place in the building. Those who oppose him will find their regime (and their temple) destroyed, while his kingdom will be established."[70] Regarding the rejection of Christ, the apostle Peter is also linked to the Psalm 118 passage in his speech to the Jewish leaders, saying "this Jesus is the stone that was rejected by you, the builders, which has become the cornerstone" (Acts 4:11).

In 1 Peter 2, this theme is expanded upon. It is said that believers are like living stones being built up as a spiritual house: "As you come to him, a living stone rejected by men but in the sight of God chosen and precious, you yourselves like living stones are being built up as a spiritual house, to be a holy priesthood, to offer spiritual sacrifices acceptable to God through Jesus Christ" (2:3–5). God has laid a cornerstone in Zion (cf. 1 Pet 2:6, citing Isaiah 28:16); this is the stone that the builders rejected but has become the cornerstone (1 Pet 2:7; Ps 118:2–3). The Psalm 118 cornerstone passage is cited in reference to the spiritual building. The word *house* (οἶκος) is used in 1 Peter 2:5 rather than *temple* (ναός), but the allusions to the temple here are quite obvious:

> The use of the word house and the emphasis in vs 9–10 on belonging to the people of God could have been a great encouragement to those who felt their position as "aliens and strangers" (2:11). Peter may have had in mind here the destruction of the temple (foretold by Jesus in Mk. 13:2). Christians individually (1 Cor 6:19) and the church corporately (1 Cor 3:16) are seen as God's new temple, a spiritual house (5) because it is indwelt by his Spirit.[71]

70. Wright, *Victory of God*, 501.
71. Wheaton, "1 Peter," 1376.

In reference to 1 Peter 2:4–9, Nicholas Perrin points out that the author of the text "found no awkwardness in simultaneously affirming, on the one side, the Christian community as temple and priesthood, and, on the other side, Christ as temple-foundation and High Priest."[72] Perrin attributes this focus to Peter's pastoral strategy during persecution in that both Christ and His followers are rejected yet precious.[73] Since the stone that the builders rejected has become the cornerstone, it should not be a surprise that the early believers are rejected as well. Peter is not taking an explicit anti-temple position; he avoids condemning the Jerusalem temple.

Some have suggested that the community of believers is only "like" the Jerusalem temple,[74] which would make it a metaphorical comparison. However, the decisive point that undercuts that position is the fact that the Holy Spirit is (in reality) seen as dwelling in this new corporate temple made up of God's people (1 Cor 3:16; Eph 2:19–22). It is not only the temple language but the language concerning the presence of God that goes with it that makes the temple transformation a new reality for the movement that followed Jesus as the Messiah. Perrin seems to be following the right path in rejecting two opposite extremes: (1) that the early believers saw themselves as being only "like" the temple in an abstract sense, and (2) that the early church "saw itself as *directly* usurping the role of the Jerusalem temple without remainder."[75] The church rejected circumcision and the yoke of the law for the Gentiles; it would be impossible for these Gentile followers of Christ to even enter the temple precincts. While Paul could still visit the temple in Jerusalem and complete a vow there, it seems correct in view of his writings to say that "Paul sees the Christian community taking the place of the temple as the eschatological temple of God, as the place where God dwells and is worshiped."[76]

---

72. Perrin, *Jesus the Temple*, 56.
73. Perrin, *Jesus the Temple*, 56.
74. Perrin, *Jesus the Temple*, 47.
75. Perrin, *Jesus the Temple*, 47.
76. Ladd, *Theology of the New Testament*, 585.

Exploring the Discontinuity

In an intertextual comparison between OT and NT texts, there is not a prediction in the OT, per se, that in the future the OT temple would *become* communities of believers who would be called the temple of God, as is found in the NT. So, how could such a wholesale change be justified by the NT apostolic community, in light of the OT texts? The passage from Psalm 118:22-23 stands out as crucial in light of the rejection of Jesus as the Jewish Messiah and his crucifixion by the Romans, by showing that what the builders rejected has become the cornerstone. Clearly, the stone that is referred to in this Psalm is not a physical stone for a physical structure. The stone that is rejected and becomes the cornerstone is a symbolic statement yet a concrete reality. The cornerstone of what building, though? In the ministry of Jesus, each of the Synoptic Gospels recounts the Parable of the Tenants shortly before his crucifixion, in which Jesus describes the rejection of the son and includes the cornerstone citation from Psalm 118:22-23. In light of the growing opposition to Jesus and his ministry, the rejected cornerstone becomes a key OT passage. In Matthew's Gospel, after the cornerstone passage from Psalm 118, Jesus adds, "therefore I tell you, the kingdom of God will be taken away from you and given to a people producing its fruits" (Matt 21:43). The rejection of the ministry of Jesus figures prominently in the Parable of the Tenants, and the citation from Psalm 118 provides an explanation of God's greater purposes, which could not be stopped by the seemingly unthinkable happening: Jesus is rejected by the national leaders as Israel's Messiah, and then crucified by the Romans. The only way for this stone to become the cornerstone, then, would be something marvelous, and of God's doing (Ps 118:23). For the early community of Jesus' followers, then, this new building began with Christ's resurrection.

Peter, in his defense before the Jewish leaders, also identifies Jesus as the stone the builders rejected who has now become the cornerstone (Acts 4:11; cf. 4:5-12). This is tied to Christ's death and resurrection in the early apostolic preaching:

Freely Gathered Communities of Faith

> Let it be known to all of you and to all the people of Israel that by the name of Jesus Christ of Nazareth, whom you crucified, whom God raised from the dead—by him this man is standing before you well. This Jesus is the stone that was rejected by you, the builders, which has become the cornerstone. And there is salvation in no one else, for there is no other name under heaven given among men by which we must be saved.[77]

The resurrection of Jesus provided the divine response to the rejection of the stone by the builders. The resurrected Christ has become the cornerstone of the entire building that God is constructing, and salvation can be found in no one else (Acts 4:12). This identifies the people of God as being completely dependent on Jesus, as the risen Messiah, for salvation. So the cornerstone is tied to salvation—the future of the people of God.

How would God build upon this cornerstone? While this is not developed in the passages in the Synoptic Gospels and Acts that refer to Psalm 118, it clearly points to a building that God will be constructing. Paul later identifies Jesus more precisely as the *cornerstone of the new temple* that God is building, composed of Jews and Gentiles (Eph 2:20; cf. 2:11–22). Clearly, by this time in Paul's understanding the cornerstone imagery had developed into a greater vision of a temple not made with hands, a temple of believers. These temples in various locations would be communities built on faith in Jesus, who were indwelt by the Holy Spirit (1 Cor 3:9–17; 2 Cor 6:15–16).

Peter also develops the cornerstone image further, in his first letter. The Messiah Jesus is the living stone that the builders rejected (1 Pet 2:4, cf. Ps 118:22). The risen Messiah is now called the living stone, pointing to his resurrection after his rejection by the builders. As believers come to him, they are also being added to the spiritual house that God is building (1 Pet 2:5).[78] Peter then adds another cornerstone passage from Isaiah 28:16: "For it stands in Scripture:

---

77. Acts 4:10–12.

78. Note that the word "house" in reference to God's house is often used interchangeably with the word "temple" in the OT (cf. Pss 5:7; 27:4; 42:4; 65:4; 69:9; 1 Kgs 5:2–5; 1 Chr 22:6–11; Jer 27:16–22).

Changes Regarding the Temple

"Behold, I am laying in Zion a stone, a cornerstone chosen and precious, and whoever believes in him will not be put to shame." (1 Pet 2:6; here Peter follows the LXX for Isaiah 28:16; whoever believes "in him" is the emphasis as seen in καὶ ὁ πιστεύων ἐπ' αὐτῷ οὐ μὴ καταισχυνθῇ). In contrast with shame, Peter emphasizes the honor of believing, saying "So the honor is for you who believe, but for those who do not believe, "The stone that the builders rejected has become the cornerstone," and "A stone of stumbling, and a rock of offense." They stumble because they disobey the word, as they were destined to do." (1 Pet 2:7-8, cf. Ps 118:22; Isa 8:14). Believing is central here, since the one who believes will not be put to shame, but will rather be honored.

Reviewing the intertextual applications of Psalm 118:22, it is clear that while the entire temple image is not fully developed in the OT as pointing to a future community of believers, the rejected stone that becomes the cornerstone is foundational for the greater temple imagery that developed.

Fulfillment of Temple Symbolism

There is a massive shift between the OT and the NT when one considers the wider context of temple references and symbolism. All of the laws and regulations concerning the OT temple are ultimately displaced by the new temple. Christ in his person fulfills the sacrificial system. Animal sacrifices are no longer necessary; all of the regulations concerning the OT temple—the sacrificial laws and offerings, the laws and regulations concerning the priesthood, the OT boundaries of sacred space, the elaborate descriptions of the temple furnishings—are transcended by the new Christ-centered temple which will exist wherever Jewish and Gentile followers of Christ are formed into communities among the nations. This expansion and availability of the presence of God in the communities of faith is founded upon the proclamation of Jesus as Messiah and Lord among the nations (Matt 28:18-20). It is a shift from God working primarily through one nation to a work that would go on among all nations in and through the new communities that are founded upon faith in Christ. The ultimate goal is the restoration of the presence of God throughout the earth, and Beale points out that "while the expansion of the church expands the presence of God in the earth through his new temple as the temple of his presence, this goal is only completely accomplished at the end of time."[79]

The emphasis on the community that is based on faith in Jesus as Messiah is tangible in the NT. The presence of God is with the new community because of the indwelling Holy Spirit; the sacrifice of Christ is now the all-sufficient sacrifice for the forgiveness of sins; the barriers between Jews and Gentiles are removed so that the believers can become one body, one temple of God; circumcision is not required for the Gentiles and water baptism becomes a key identity marker for the new movement. Older markers are removed so that communities of faith in Christ can be freely formed among all nations.

---

79. Beale, *New Testament Biblical Theology*, 648.

7

Contrasts between the Old Testament Nation and the New Testament Communities of Faith in Christ

FREELY GATHERED COMMUNITIES

Freely gathered communities based on faith in Christ become the new paradigm in the NT canonical texts. The new communities of faith provide a clear contrast with the emphasis on a chosen nation in the OT. As these new communities are established in various locations in the Greco-Roman world, they are not given land promises or the use of the sword to establish physical territories for the people of God. They are not on a crusade to capture land, and they have no warrant to establish a human government over any nation. The NT communities of faith that are established in Israel also do not attempt to wrest control of the nation from the Roman government, and at no point do they gain the religious control of the nation by taking it from the religious leaders in Jerusalem.

The lack of control they had over the governmental or religious leadership structures and the lack of control they had over any national territory highlights the fact that they were freely gathered communities professing an allegiance to Jesus as Messiah. These communities that were founded on faith in Christ were the essence of what God was establishing in the NT. These communities were "freely gathered" because they were built on a response to the message of Christ (Col 1:24-29). As such they were founded on faith in the resurrected Christ (Rom 10:8-10; 1 Cor 15). Key points regarding the establishment of these communities are: (1) Jesus was proclaimed as Lord and Messiah (2 Cor 4:5; Rom 10:8-15; Acts 2:36); (2) repentance toward God and faith in Jesus Christ was proclaimed (Acts 20:20-21); (3) open communication of the truth was used to persuade others to believe (2 Cor 4:2; 2 Cor 5:10-11); (4) those who believed were baptized in water and added to the community of faith (Acts 2:38-41; 8:12; 16:31-34); (5) the reception and empowerment of the Spirit also established the fact that the Spirit of God was now with the followers of Christ, and these communities became known as the temple of God (Acts 2:1-17; 1 Cor 3:16-17); (6) faith was foundational for the new temple God was building. Being saved by grace through faith is a foundational statement (Eph 2:8-9), and Paul goes on in the same passage to describe the Gentiles being added to the temple along with the Jewish believers (Eph 2:10-22); (7) believing resulted in salvation, as well as fellowship within the body of believers (Acts 16:29-33; 2:38-42). It was above all a spiritual movement, yet it had many practical and social ramifications as well. Although there was conflict for a time regarding the inclusion of the Gentiles, eventually it became clear that both Jews and Gentiles could be added to these communities based on faith in Jesus as Messiah and Lord (Acts 10:1-11:18; 15:1-31; Rom 10:5-13).

It is this freely gathered community paradigm that provides the explanation for many of the discontinuities between the OT and NT, particularly as united with the understanding that these communities were based on faith in Jesus as Messiah. This paradigm shift coincided with a central focus of the NT: that Jesus was indeed the Messiah and had fulfilled the prophetic predictions and vision of the OT writings. The thesis identifies the NT communities as "freely gathered communities of faith in Christ, composed of Jews

CONTRASTS BETWEEN THE OLD TESTAMENT NATION

and Gentiles." So while the freely gathered communities provide part of the paradigm shift, the other part (central to OT and NT texts) is that of faith in Jesus as Messiah and Lord.

Jesus and the New Communities of Faith

Jesus provided key aspects for these communities of faith; they were not just a later Pauline invention. There are ways in which Jesus laid the groundwork for the new communities in his own teaching and ministry. It has been noted that the Gospels present Jesus as bringing about a renewed Israel around his own person, and that the calling of the twelve was one of his major symbolic actions.[1] Jesus brought transformation by "gathering about himself a new Israel, representative of all that the earlier Israel was ever intended to be, establishing it upon the foundation of apostles and prophets, with himself as its chief cornerstone."[2]

Jesus gathers Israel around his own person in other ways in the gospels. A radical statement is that relationship with him is more important than family relationships, in that "whoever loves father or mother more than me is not worthy of me, and whoever loves son or daughter more than me is not worthy of me" (Matt 10:37). Clearly, this shows that loyalty to him must supersede family ties (cf. Luke 14:26). His mother and brothers are those who hear the word of God and do it (Luke 8:18–21). Commenting on these and other similar sayings of Jesus that were highly unusual in that time period, N. T. Wright notes that "he envisaged loyalty to himself and his kingdom-movement as creating an alternative family."[3] Even Gentiles who have faith would come from east and west and sit down with Abraham, Isaac, and Jacob in the kingdom of God (Matt 8:5–13), demonstrating that this community would be open to those beyond the borders of Israel.

Another relational redefinition concerning Jesus is seen in the parable of the vine and the branches in John 15. In the OT Israel is

1. Wright, *How God Became King*, 196–97.
2. Woudstra, "Israel and the Church," 4778–79.
3. Wright, *Victory of God*, 401.

portrayed as the vine (Isa 5:1–7; Ps 80:8; Isa 27:2–6), but in John 15 Jesus is the vine and his followers are the branches, focusing God's people around abiding in Jesus.[4] In John 15 "Jesus is changing the place of rootedness for Israel."[5] It will not be sufficient to be living in the land; without attachment to Jesus the branches will be cast out.[6] Rather than a focus on the land, blessing now flows through Jesus and fruitfulness comes by abiding in him.[7]

The emphasis on faith that is so foundational for the new communities traces back to the ministry of Jesus. The Gospel of Mark presents the beginning of Jesus' message as "the time is fulfilled, and the kingdom of God is at hand; repent and believe in the gospel" (Mark 1:15). Believing and being saved are connected in the parable of the sower (Luke 8:11–12). The sinful woman who wept at Jesus' feet was told that her sins were forgiven (Luke 7:48), and then "your faith has saved you; go in peace" (7:50). Faith is connected with healing in numerous instances (cf. Mark 5:25–34; 10:46–52; Luke 17:11–19); this includes the healing of a Roman centurion's servant along with the intimation of the centurion's salvation (Matt 8:5–13), as well as the healing of a Canaanite woman's daughter (Matt 15:22–28). It also includes the exercise of faith in connection with the miraculous (Matt 8:23–27) and answers to prayer (Mark 11:20–24). The Gospel of John presents sayings of Jesus that connect faith in him with eternal life (6:25–40; 3:9–18; 14:1–6; 17:1–24; cf. also Luke 23:39–43). The point of mentioning these widespread attestations (along with others that could be listed) is to identify the ministry of Jesus as laying the groundwork for the believing community that followed him. This includes faith in the person of Jesus that is connected with eternal life.

---

4. Burge, *Jesus and the Land*, 1112–21; cf. John 15:1–16.
5. Burge, *Jesus and the Land*, 1113.
6. Burge, *Jesus and the Land*, 1116.
7. Martin, *Promised Land*, 130.

Christ as Key to Continuity and Discontinuity

Jesus Christ must be seen as central to both matters of continuity and discontinuity between the OT and NT.[8] Continuity is seen in that various Messianic passages in the OT are shown by the NT writers as having been fulfilled in Christ. There is one people of God and Christ himself provides continuity between the people of God in the OT and the NT. Although there is a major change when the Gentiles are incorporated into the people of God through faith in Christ, this is not a replacement of the OT people of God by the NT church. Instead there was a renewal and transformation of the people of God, and Wright notes that "the gospels themselves were written from and to communities of Jesus's followers, who believed that in Jesus as Israel's Messiah this renewal had become actual. Israel had not been abandoned. It had not been 'replaced.' It had been transformed."[9]

There is also discontinuity that is centered in Christ, in terms of fulfillment. Christ removed "the law of commandments expressed in ordinances, that he might create in himself one new man in place of the two, so making peace" (Eph 2:15; cf. 2:11–14). Through the cross both Jew and Gentile are reconciled to God in one body (Eph 2:16). The barriers between Jews and Gentiles in the OT were removed by the cross so that God could form a unified body through faith in Christ, "creating one new man in place of the two" (Eph 2:15), a reference to Jews and Gentiles as can be seen in the context (Eph. 2:11–22). Circumcision, food laws, Sabbath laws, and temple regulations are no longer required for believers now that Christ has come.[10]

KEY ASPECTS OF THE COMMUNITIES OF FAITH

The freely gathered communities of faith in Christ had key boundaries and identity markers. Rather than an exhaustive study, crucial markers identified here will include faith in Christ, the reception of

---

8. Baker, *Two Testaments, One Bible*, 270–75.
9. Wright, *How God Became King*, 196–97.
10. Schreiner, "The Commands of God," 93.

the Spirit, love, holiness, water baptism, and the Lord's Supper. In addition, another mark of the new communities was actually the *absence* of something: the removal of various ancient social barriers because of believers' inclusion "in Christ."

Social Barriers Transcended

NT communities of faith in Christ were to enter into a unity of the Holy Spirit that transcended major social barriers in the ancient world: barriers between Jews and Gentiles, slaves and free, male and female, rich and poor. (Gal 3:25-28; 1 Cor 12:13; Col 3:11; Rom 10:12-13; Jas 2:1-9). The church is the *ekklēsia*, and when used of believer it represents the assembly of the people of God "having the connotation that it is an assembly of believers who are 'fellow-citizens with God's people' [the saints] (Eph 2:19)."[11] While the word *ekklēsia* is also used of other gatherings of people in the Greco-Roman world, "what distinguished this *ekklēsia* from others was its incorporation into Jesus Christ."[12] Believers in the early communities "saw themselves as part of a family, a family that included people of different backgrounds, ethnicities, social and economic status."[13]

Faith in Christ

In the Christian communities, faith in Christ is a central identity marker of the community members: "The chief feature of this new identity is faith in Christ, which binds community members together, mitigating the differences that divide them and creating new elements that unite them. Paul constantly emphasized that every Christian, whether Jew or Gentile, lives a new reality 'in Christ'..."[14] Salvation is not through the law but through faith in Christ (Rom 3:19-28). Since salvation is by faith in Christ (Eph 2:8-9) and Christ is proclaimed to all, membership in the community is also

11. Horton, *Acts*, 7550-52.
12. Thompson, *The Church according to Paul*, 33.
13. Trebilco, "Early Christian Communities," 38.
14. Karakolis, "Formation of the Pauline Communities," 377.

available to all who believe. James Thompson notes that "faith that Jesus died and arose (1 Thess 4:14) unites them and separates them from the synagogue and from the rest of society."[15] This separation is not a physical separation but a distinction based on belief (2 Cor 4:3-4; 6:15; 1 Cor 7:13-15; 10:27). The term "believer" is a badge of identity in the new community, and "also signifies the boundary separating the community from the rest of society."[16]

The Reception of the Spirit

The Holy Spirit in the body of Christ and in each of Christ's followers assumes a central role. Reception of the Spirit is what marks the beginning of the Christian movement (Acts 2). In Acts 2 the Spirit had come "to initiate the church into the eschatological unity of an ethnically reconciled, cross-cultural people of God in the midst of the present age."[17] While the church initially had some difficulties with the barriers between Jews and Gentiles, "those truly obedient to the Spirit were ultimately forced to cross ethnic boundaries."[18] Reception of the Spirit is a key and distinct identity marker for the early Christian community, along with water baptism (Acts 2:38-39; 10:36-48; 19:1-7). The ultimate purpose of the empowerment of the Spirit was to bear witness to Jesus to the ends of the earth (Acts 1:6-8). Discontinuity between the OT and NT "lies in the fact that the people of God are no longer so on the basis of "nation," but on the basis of individual entry through faith in Jesus Christ and the gift of the Spirit, signaled by baptism."[19] The reception of the Spirit shows that the Spirit is a distinct gift to be received by faith (Acts 2:36-39; Gal 3:1-14). The gift of the Spirit empowers the church to witness to Christ (Acts 1:8). The gift of the Spirit means that the new temple is not just a loose metaphor or vague comparison with the OT temple; the Holy Spirit actually indwells the NT temple (1 Cor 3:9-16).

15. Thompson, *The Church according to Paul*, 47.
16. Thompson, *The Church according to Paul*, 34.
17. Keener, *Spirit in the Gospels and Acts*, 194.
18. Keener, *Spirit in the Gospels and Acts*, 194.
19. Fee, *People of God*, 64.

Love in the New Communities

Love was to be a central quality of the followers of Jesus (John 13:35). In cooperation with the believer the Holy Spirit would develop the fruit of the Spirit and the preeminent fruit is love (Gal 5:22-23). This love fulfills the law (Rom 13:8-10; Gal 5:14) and constitutes the central focus of Jesus in relation to the commandments (Mark 12:28-31).

The two greatest commandments identified by Jesus which summarize all of the law and the prophets are from the Pentateuch (Deut 6:4-5; Lev 19:18; Matt 22:34-40). These two commandments are based on love, which makes love central to the entire OT according to Jesus. This focus on love is also further developed in the NT. In John 15:12-13, Jesus gives a definition of love that is sacrificial: "This is my commandment, that you love one another as I have loved you. Greater love has no one than this, that someone lay down his life for his friends." Here Jesus provides the incarnational example and definition of love, as a willingness to sacrifice on behalf of others for their own well-being. This sacrificial love is to be imitated by Christ's followers (Eph 5:1-2). As a central aspect of the communities of faith, love would be needed in order to cross social, ethnic, class and other barriers and provide a basis of fellowship for Christ's followers.

Holiness

Holiness was also a central reality for the NT communities (cf. 1 Pet 1:14-16; Eph 2:19-22; Col 1:19-22). The church is the temple of the Holy Spirit and the presence of God defines the holiness of the church (1 Cor 3:16-17; 2 Cor 6:14-7:1). In Paul's theology holiness is a central aspect of Christ's communities of faith in that: "(1) holiness is difference from the life of Gentile non-believers; (2) holiness is both the character and the activity of the triune God; and (3) holiness is essentially Christ-likeness."[20] Holiness is the work of the Holy Spirit. This starts with the work of the Spirit

---

20. Gorman, "You Shall Be Cruciform," 153; cf. 2 Cor 6:14-18; Eph 5:1-2; Col 3:9-15.

Contrasts between the Old Testament Nation

in "bringing adoption as sons and daughters of God."[21] The divine calling marks Christ's followers as belonging to God, which means that they share in his holiness.[22]

A major discontinuity with the OT is that many holiness markers, such as clean and unclean food laws, temple regulations regarding holy spaces, and other ritual boundaries are no longer required laws because the new communities of faith include Jews and Gentiles and the believing community is the new temple of God. While Jewish followers of Christ could still choose to follow Jewish customs such as keeping the Sabbath or eating certain foods, these customs were not to be imposed on the entire community (Rom 14:1-6). Gentile believers were not to despise Jewish cultural practices, either. Commenting on Romans 14:1—15:6, Keener notes that "Gentile believers must not look down on Jewish people's food customs or holy days."[23] The importance of Jewish and Gentile believers being able to recline at table and fellowship together is a key pattern of social praxis that Paul fought for (Gal 2:11-16).

The holiness emphasis on God's presence is retained in NT teaching (2 Cor 6:16-18), and there is still a separation that is emphasized. This is seen in Paul's admonition to the Corinthian believers (2 Cor 6:17-7:1). But in the context of Paul's writings this must be regarded as a call to separation from sinful practices, not a separation from social interaction with unbelievers.[24] Intertextual comparison shows that the adoption of temple terminology in the NT is a major change, with the NT temple-communities being identified as God's temple as well as the presence of God and holiness being linked to this temple (1 Cor 3:16-17; Eph 2:11-22; 2 Cor 6:16—7:1; cf. 1 Kgs 8:6-13; 2 Chron 5:7-7:3; Pss 5:7; 11:4).

---

21. Oakes, "Made Holy by the Holy Spirit," 183.
22. Oakes, "Made Holy by the Holy Spirit," 173-74.
23. Keener, "One New Temple in Christ," 87.
24. cf. 1 Cor 5:9-10.

Water Baptism

Water baptism was a key identity marker for the early church. To those who received the message in Acts 2, Peter's instructions were to repent and be baptized in water (2:38). Water baptism is identified as an essential aspect of proclaiming the gospel and making disciples (Matt 28:18–20; Mark 16:15–16; Acts 2:38; 22:12–16). Paul identifies the symbolism of water baptism as pointing to a participation in the death and resurrection of Christ (Rom 6:1–11). Water baptism provided a physical enactment of identification with Christ as a public testimony to one's faith in Christ. Water baptism was a symbol of unity and of inclusion in Christ for the community of faith.

The Lord's Supper and the New Covenant

Paul's instructions to the Corinthian church identify the Lord's Supper with the Passover meal celebrated by Christ and his disciples and identify the cup as the cup of the new covenant in Christ's blood (1 Cor 11:25; Luke 22:7–20). The new covenant reference is a major marker for early Christianity, identifying the Christian community as participating in the new covenant promised by Jeremiah (31:31–34). The author of Hebrews writes that this new covenant includes not only the forgiveness of sins but the promise that God would write his laws on their hearts and minds (Heb 10:16–17; 8:6–13; Jer 31:33). Participation in the Lord's Supper in connection with the new covenant is an identifying practice for Christ's followers.

Torah and Nation

The Torah provides the land boundaries, theological support, civil and moral laws, cultural boundaries, cultic system, and other markers for the nation of Israel. The various OT laws helped insure their survival as a nation until the coming of Christ.[25] For the NT communities of faith in Christ, the first five books of the OT (along with the rest of the OT writings) are the things written in the past for our

---

25. Cotton, *Studying the Old Testament*, 27.

Contrasts between the Old Testament Nation

instruction (1 Cor 10:11) and are still viewed as Scripture.[26] But the focus shifts to faith in Christ as the complete ground of acceptance with God for both Jews and Gentiles, and the inner empowerment of the Holy Spirit is stressed as a new covenant promise to enable fulfillment of God's laws that have been written on the heart (Rom 8:3–13). Moral, ethical, and spiritual exhortations permeate the NT writings. But it is the empowerment of the Spirit that enables the fulfillment of Christian ethics.[27] Christ's followers are not under law, but under grace (Rom 6:14).

The people of God in the OT are not replaced by the church; instead, the people of God are widened in the NT communities to include both Jews and Gentiles who have faith in Jesus as Messiah (Gal 3:25–29). The Lord's Supper and water baptism become the central ordinances of the NT communities and are reflective of believers being included in Christ's death and resurrection both individually and corporately.

Praxis

The change from the OT nation of Israel to the NT communities of faith had a crucial pragmatic dimension when viewed as the development of God's plan for reaching the nations. The NT communities of faith were the new strategy, the new societal unit that would become the vehicle for the message of Christ and the work of spiritual transformation for God's people as accomplished by the Spirit of God among the nations. The physical realities of land and sword, circumcision, food laws, ceremonial laws, and enforced civil laws, while necessary for God's purposes in protecting the integrity of Israel as a nation over many centuries, are set aside for the next stage in God's plan.

---

26. Thielman, *The Law and the New Testament*, 35.
27. Fee, *People of God*, 105.

8

The Paradigm Shift and its Implications for Today

REVIEW OF FINDINGS

Two contrasting organizational paradigms can be seen for the divine purposes in the canonical writings: the OT nation of Israel, and the freely gathered communities of faith in Christ in the NT. The contrasts between them explains many of the discontinuities between the OT and NT. The themes of land, sword, and temple have been examined in light of this thesis, which has been shown to provide a clarifying explanation for the changes that took place and a synthesis that joins these themes together. The thesis states that "many of the discontinuities between the OT and the NT can be best explained as the differences between God's instructions for a nation in the OT, and God's instructions for freely gathered communities of faith in Christ in the NT."

Land, sword, and temple have been traced to show how the discontinuities in these themes from OT to NT can be explained by the thesis. A summary overview presents many discontinuities that are covered:

The Paradigm Shift and its Implications for Today

- The OT nation has a temple that is required by the Torah; the NT communities of faith become the temple of God.

- The OT temple has animal sacrifices; Jesus Christ in the NT fulfills all sacrifices; in the NT temple–community, no further animal sacrifices are offered.

- The OT temple is constructed with various laws and regulations concerning holy spaces and how to relate to God's presence. These regulations are designed to emphasize God's holiness, God's presence, and the people's devotion to God. In the NT temple, the OT temple regulations are set aside. Jewish and Gentile believers are joined together and the community of faith is the temple of the Holy Spirit. Holiness is still emphasized in terms of the presence of God in the new temple, along with ethical and relational purity.

- The OT priesthood with its various regulations and ordinances is required for presenting animal sacrifices at the temple; this priesthood is no longer needed for the NT communities of faith.

- The various laws that separated Jews and Gentiles in the OT—circumcision, food laws, and Sabbath laws—are set aside as requirements for the NT communities of faith since the new temple is composed of Jews and Gentiles.

- The OT nation is given the sword for obtaining the Promised Land, while the NT communities are told to put away the sword. They have no warrant to take Promised Lands by the sword as new communities are planted in the Greco–Roman world.

- The OT nation is given the sword for national defense; the NT communities flee from persecution rather than resisting enemies by use of the sword. They are told to love their enemies and to be faithful unto death. Intertextual comparison shows this to be a striking change across the Testaments.

- The OT nation is given the sword to enforce various societal laws in the Torah (recognizing that the death penalty was enforced by more than one method); in the NT, rather than using the death penalty for violations of OT commandments, they only remove the unrepentant sinner from the community through excommunication.

- The emphasis on the Promised Land in the OT is expanded to include the entire world and is transformed in the NT. Rather than any kind of land conquest, the ultimate inheritance is the new heavens and the new earth in the age to come. In the NT, Christ is the heir of all things and replaces the OT focus on land.

The above list covers quite a significant number of discontinuities between the OT and the NT, which are explained by the thesis. The thesis may provide an explanation for additional discontinuities, beyond the ones presented here in relation to land, sword, and the temple.

The themes of land, sword, and temple have been examined in light of the canonical texts and contemporary scholarship. I have sought to indicate my indebtedness to contemporary scholars regarding the themes of land, sword, and temple with the various citations and references indicated in the study. This research has resulted in a growing appreciation for the work of numerous authors as well as an awareness of progress that has been made. The progress in examining the theme of land from OT to NT, for example, has shed new light on changes between the OT and NT which have been referenced and incorporated into this study.

The most significant point of this study, however, has been to examine the themes of land, sword, and temple in relation to the thesis, which can then be used to explain additional discontinuities between the OT and NT. It is the freely gathered communities of faith in Christ (composed of Jews and Gentiles) which provides the explanation for the discontinuities, when contrasted with the OT nation. While the freely gathered communities in the NT provide part of this paradigm shift as shown in the thesis, the other part (central to OT and NT texts) is that of faith in Jesus as Messiah and Lord. The focus on the crucified and risen Lord is the center of the new communities. Faith in this crucified and risen Messiah and Lord is the *sine qua non* of the new communities, which then leads to the reception and empowerment of the Holy Spirit (Acts 2:1–41; 8:5–17; 10:34–48). Salvation is by faith in Christ alone, by God's

The Paradigm Shift and its Implications for Today

grace alone (Eph 2:8–9). The Word of God points to Jesus Christ and leads individuals to faith in him. The new communities of faith provide the crucial contrast with key features of the OT nation, in order to explain discontinuities.

RECOMMENDATIONS FOR FURTHER RESEARCH

The thesis may offer a perspective to shed light on additional discontinuities between the OT and NT, which is a key aspect of this study. For example, regarding changes in leadership and ministry: how do changes in leadership relate to the thesis? How does the OT prophet differ in his (or her) ministry to the OT nation, as compared with the NT prophet that addresses freely gathered communities of faith? Or, how does the office of priest change from OT nation to NT communities of faith? How does kingship change? There are studies that have addressed these changes from various angles, but the question is, how might the thesis provide more clarity in terms of an explanation for these discontinuities and a correlation with other discontinuities?

Kingship is developed over time in the OT to provide leadership to the OT nation, but the focus of the OT prophets includes messianic kingship for Israel's future. In the NT, this kingship is fulfilled in Jesus as Messiah. The NT communities of faith, freed from dependence on a physical land or a single nation, look to the resurrected Jesus as Messiah and Lord. How does this transformation relate to the change from OT nation to NT communities of faith, and what are the wider implications of this change? The thesis may provide additional clarity by correlating these changes with the other discontinuities that have been examined.

Another current focal point is the intense debate on changes in the role of the Law from OT to NT. The change to NT communities of faith in Christ composed of Jews and Gentiles has already been shown to be a major factor in setting aside the laws of separation between Jews and Gentiles, as is referenced in this study. While beyond the scope of this study, it is possible that additional insight regarding the Law could still be gained by the contrast between OT nation and freely gathered communities of faith in Christ, particularly as these communities were empowered by the Spirit.

Additional cultural markers of the OT nation are no longer directly applied in the NT communities, which may relate to the thesis. Agricultural instructions to leave the gleanings at the edges of the field (Lev 19:9–10) would not work in a number of countries today, where the poor are in urban areas that are widely separated from farm lands. The principle of caring for the poor can be drawn from these OT examples, however, and applied to today.[1] It is a fascinating fact of history to consider all of the ANE cultural and religious practices of the OT nation that are left behind (including all the points previously addressed in this study) so that the NT communities of faith can move freely into various countries throughout the world.

A more complete enumeration of agricultural laws, civil laws, and other social laws that apply to the OT nation can be added to what has been addressed here on the OT side, and contrasted with what is made applicable to the NT communities of faith. This would expand the usefulness of the thesis to cover a broader number of discontinuities. In many cases there are principles which can be drawn from OT practices even when the cultural practices themselves no longer apply. In addition, of course, there are the doctrinal and ethical teachings that carry over to the NT and to today (cf. 1 Cor 10:1–11; Rom 15:1–4). The many areas of continuity, along with areas of development in divine revelation across the OT and NT canonical texts, could be added to the explanation of discontinuities utilized in the thesis in order to develop a more complete and comprehensive biblical theology that can be better understood in contemporary cultures.

---

1. Cotton, *Studying the Old Testament*, 38–39.

The Paradigm Shift and its Implications for Today

LIMITATIONS TO THE STUDY

The Development of a Complete Biblical Theology

This study has not been an attempt to develop a complete biblical theology. The focus of the thesis has been identifying and explaining discontinuities; a full biblical theology must at least address continuities, discontinuities, and areas of development or progress in divine revelation when moving across the entire biblical canon.

A full biblical theology examines the Torah, the Prophets, and the Writings of the OT to see how each contributes in its own unique way to God's instructions for the OT nation; each of the NT canonical texts can be examined for how they contribute specific dimensions of God's instructions for the freely gathered communities of faith in Christ.

Ecclesiology

The word "church" has inherited a great deal of Western baggage, much of which took place as a result of the joining of church and state which began with the impetus of the Roman Emperor, Constantine, and continued to grow and develop into the Middle Ages. This Western baggage has tended to obscure the actual change that was taking place. "Freely gathered communities of faith in Christ" is more descriptive of the actual paradigm shift that took place, a radical shift which enabled Christianity to spread through the ancient world in a remarkable way, particularly when tied to the empowerment and life of the Spirit.

These communities were based on faith in Christ rather than ethnicity, social status, or wealth. Barriers between Jews and Gentiles, slaves and free, male and female, rich and poor were removed "in Christ" (Gal 3:25-28). The Day of Pentecost is the beginning point for the Spirit being poured out on all flesh, and the unity of the Spirit that is demonstrated there continues to grow in Acts as the Spirit joins believers together in the new communities of faith. A limitation of the research here is that there was not an attempt to outline a fully developed ecclesiology; only key areas have been developed in relation to the NT communities in contrast with the OT nation, based on the three themes that were covered.

REFLECTIONS AND IMPLICATIONS

The community emphasis of the NT is very significant. These are *communities* of faith; this cuts against the Western individualism that has become so prevalent in modern societies. The communities of faith are also not a *nation*; this cuts against any form of nationalism as well as attempts to advance the kingdom of God by force.

Communities of faith in Christ could survive and thrive in a pagan Roman Empire. They were not derailed by persecution, Roman corruption, or competing religious or philosophical voices. The early believers did not try to dominate others through the use of force, or by capturing the control of human governments. In this they provide a powerful example. They loved one another and invited people of all backgrounds to a fellowship in Christ that exhibited the fruit of the Spirit, fruit which was very appealing.

Today, rather than churches attempting to control national governments as a means of leveraging power, it is crucial that the boundaries of NT teaching be kept intact in order to safeguard the Christian communities of faith. This is true regardless of the culture in which Christ's followers are located. This is so that faith in Christ, love for one another, and the fruit of the Spirit can flourish and bring a widening circle of influence to impact the world.

The church cannot touch the sword, and has damaged its witness when it has done so in episodes such as the Crusades and the Inquisition of the Middle Ages. The clear distinction between the OT nation and the NT church is crucial in this area. Nationalism, syncretism with pagan culture, racism, materialism, violence in the name of religion: all of these practices have at times corrupted the witness and influence of the church. These corrupting idols can only be countered by fidelity to NT teaching.

The many changes between the OT and NT are often a source of confusion and misunderstanding for the average person who reads the Bible. The fruit of accurate biblical scholarship should

THE PARADIGM SHIFT AND ITS IMPLICATIONS FOR TODAY

not be limited to conversations among scholars, but should seek to clarify biblical teachings for people in general inasmuch as this is possible. The thesis can provide an organizational principle for explaining discontinuities between the OT and NT, and undoubtedly much more work needs to be done in this area.

CONCLUSION

Addressing and explaining discontinuities between the Testaments has been a key issue that Christ's followers have wrestled with since the early centuries of Christianity. In the post-apostolic era, the impact of Greek culture influenced the church to embrace allegory to explain difficult texts, which led them away from the original author's intended meaning. Today, there are very different cultural influences which seek to confuse and undermine accurate biblical interpretation in the area of explaining discontinuities: predisposing influences such as Western skepticism, anti-supernaturalism, and secular humanism. On the positive side, new work is being done in this area of biblical scholarship, and there is a great opportunity to address discontinuities in better ways than have been done in the past.

An advantage of focusing on discontinuities in a comparison between God's instructions for OT Israel and God's instructions for NT communities of faith in Christ is that one can utilize this comparison and be faithful to the contextual meaning of the canonical texts while also analyzing the influence of divine inspiration across the Testaments. There is also a Christ-centered focus that is emphasized in this approach: the NT communities were based on faith in Christ, and the NT texts focus on Jesus Christ as Messiah and Lord.

Discontinuities between the OT and NT involve complex areas of theology and praxis, the revelation of Jesus as the Messiah, and the long range plan of God in restoring humanity to himself. God's ultimate purpose of reconciling the world to himself through Christ (2 Cor. 5:18-19) and developing a people in his own image (Col. 1:15; Rom. 8:29) are central to God's overall strategy. The OT nation prepares the way and sets the stage for the coming of Christ;

Freely Gathered Communities of Faith

Christ's death and resurrection provide the message of salvation for all nations. The massive shift from God's instructions for the OT nation of Israel to the freely gathered NT communities of faith in Christ provides the greatest number of explanations for the discontinuities between the OT and NT, and includes major changes in praxis and theology. Theological changes are based on Christ's fulfillment of the divine purposes regarding the OT nation of Israel, and the reality of Christ's death and resurrection for the salvation of all who believe. Changes in praxis accompany changes in theology and build on the foundation of the inclusion of Jews and Gentiles in the body of Christ which would exist as freely gathered communities of faith in Christ among all nations. These freely gathered communities would leave behind a large number of cultural markers, the OT civil laws, various ANE customs, and key religious practices found in the Torah so that the freely gathered communities of faith could function well as Christ's body in the diverse cultures of the world.

Bibliography

Alexander, T. Desmond. "Beyond Borders: The Wider Dimensions of the Land." In *The Land of Promise: Biblical, Theological, and Contemporary Perspectives*, edited by Philip Johnston and Peter Walker, 35–50. Downers Grove: InterVarsity, 2000.

———. *From Eden to the New Jerusalem: An Introduction to Biblical Theology*. Grand Rapids: Kregel, 2008.

———. *From Paradise to the Promised Land: An Introduction to the Pentateuch*. 3rd ed. Grand Rapids: Baker Academic, 2012.

Averbeck, R. E. "Tabernacle." In *DOTP*, edited by T. Desmond Alexander and David W. Baker, 807–27. Downers Grove: InterVarsity, 2003.

Bahnsen, Greg L. "The Theonomic Reformed Approach to the Law and Gospel." In *The Law, the Gospel, and the Modern Christian: Five Views*, edited by Wayne G. Strickland. 93–143. Grand Rapids: Zondervan, 1993.

Baker, David L. *Two Testaments, One Bible: The Theological Relationship between the Old and New Testaments*. 3rd ed. Downers Grove: InterVarsity, 2010.

Barnett, Paul. *Jesus & the Rise of Early Christianity: A History of New Testament Times*. Downers Grove: InterVarsity, 1999.

Beale, G. K. *Handbook on the New Testament Use of the Old Testament: Exegesis and Interpretation*. Grand Rapids: Baker Academic, 2012.

———. *A New Testament Biblical Theology*. Grand Rapids: Baker Academic, 2011.

———. *The Temple and the Church's Mission: A Biblical Theology of the Dwelling Place of God*. Downers Grove: InterVarsity, 2004.

Blomberg, Craig L., Robert L. Hubbard, and William W. Klein. *Introduction to Biblical Interpretation*. Rev. ed. Dallas: Word, 2004.

Borg, Marcus J. *Conflict, Holiness and Politics in the Teachings of Jesus*. 2nd ed. Harrisburg: Trinity, 1998.

Boyd, Gregory A. *Crucifixion of the Warrior God: Interpreting the Old Testament's Violent Portraits of God in Light of the Cross*. Minneapolis: Fortress, 2017.

Brandon, Samuel G. F. *Jesus and the Zealots: A Study of the Political Factor in Primitive Christianity*. New York: Scribner's, 1967.

Brenneman, Laura L., and Brad D. Schantz, eds. *Struggles for Shalom: Peace and Violence across the Testaments*. Eugene, OR: Pickwick, 2014.

Bibliography

Brownlee, W. H. "From Holy War to Holy Martyrdom." In *The Quest for the Kingdom of God: Studies in Honor of George E. Mendenhall*, edited by A. R. W. Green et al., 286–92. Winona Lake, IN: Eisenbrauns, 1983.

Brueggemann, Walter. *The Land: Place as Gift, Promise, and Challenge in Biblical Faith*. 2nd ed. Minneapolis: Fortress, 2002. (1st ed. 1977).

Burge, Gary M. *Jesus and the Land: The New Testament Challenge to "Holy Land" Theology*. Grand Rapids: Baker Academic, 2010. Kindle.

Calvin, John. *Commentary on a Harmony of the Evangelists, Matthew, Mark and Luke*. Vol. 3. Translated by William Pringle. 1846. http://www.biblestudyguide.org/ebooks/comment/calcom33.pdf

Chamberlin, Knox. "The Law of Moses and the Law of Christ." In *Continuity and Discontinuity (Essays in Honor of S. Lewis Johnson, Jr.): Perspectives on the Relationship between the Old and New Testaments*, edited by John S. Feinberg, 3677–4169. Wheaton: Crossway, 1988. Kindle.

Chapman, Stephen B. "Martial Memory, Peaceable Vision: Divine War in the Old Testament." In *Holy War in the Bible: Christian Morality and an Old Testament Problem*, edited by Paul Copan et al., 47–67. Downers Grove: IVP Academic, 2013.

Chilton, Bruce. "Temple, Jewish." In *DNTB*, edited by Stanley E. Porter and Craig A. Evans, 1167–83. Downers Grove: IVP Academic, 2000.

Chingota, Felix L. "Leviticus." In *Africa Bible Commentary*, edited by Tokunboh Adeyemo, 89. 2nd ed. Grand Rapids: Zondervan, 2010.

Christiansen, Ellen Juhl. *The Covenant and its Ritual Boundaries in Palestinian Judaism and Pauline Christianity*. Durham doctoral theses, Durham University, 1993. http://etheses.dur.ac.uk/5801/.

Copan, Paul, and Matthew Flannagan. *Did God Really Command Genocide? Coming to Terms with the Justice of God*. Grand Rapids: Baker, 2014.

———. "The Ethics of "Holy War" for Christian Morality and Theology." In *Holy War in the Bible: Christian Morality and an Old Testament Problem*, edited by Paul Copan et al., 201–39. Downers Grove: InterVarsity, 2013.

Cothey, Antony. "Ethics and Holiness in the Theology of Leviticus." *JSOT* 30.2 (2005) 131–51.

Cotton, Roger D. "Essential Truths of Old Testament Theology." In *The Pentateuch: Critical Issues, Readings and Resource Materials*, 81–83. Springfield, MO: Global University, 2011.

———. "Holiness." In *The Pentateuch: Critical Issues, Readings and Resource Materials*, 97–98. Springfield, MO: Global University, 2011.

———. *Studying the Old Testament: Principles and Techniques*. Springfield, MO: Global University, 2015.

———. "The Tabernacle." In *The Pentateuch: Critical Issues, Readings and Resource Materials*, 92–94. Springfield, MO: Global University, 2011.

———. "Understanding the Sabbath." In *The Pentateuch: Critical Issues, Readings and Resource Materials*, 91–92. Springfield, MO: Global University, 2011.

———. "Universal Principles of the Law." In *The Pentateuch: Critical Issues, Readings and Resource Materials*, 89–90. Springfield, MO: Global University, 2011.

Davies, W. D. *The Gospel and the Land: Early Christianity and Jewish Territorial Doctrine*. Berkley: University of California Press, 1974.

deSilva, David A. *Honor, Patronage, Kinship and Purity: Unlocking New Testament Culture*. Downers Grove: InterVarsity, 2000.

Demarest, Bruce A., and Gordon R. Lewis. *Integrative Theology*, vol. 3. Grand Rapids: Zondervan, 1994.

Dempster, Stephen G. *Dominion and Dynasty: A Theology of the Hebrew Bible*. New Studies in Biblical Theology 15. Downers Grove: InterVarsity, 2003. Kindle.

Dunn, James D. G. *The Parting of the Ways: Between Christianity and Judaism and their Significance for the Character of Christianity*. Philadelphia: Trinity, 1991.

Elliot, John H. "Temple versus Household in Luke–Acts: A Contrast in Social Institutions." In *The Social World of Luke–Acts: Models for Interpretation*, edited by Jerome H. Neyrey, 211–40. Peabody, MA: Hendrickson, 1991.

Fee, Gordon D. *Paul, the Spirit, and the People of God*. Peabody, MA: Hendrickson, 1996.

Feinberg, John S. "Systems of Discontinuity." In *Continuity and Discontinuity (Essays in Honor of S. Lewis Johnson, Jr.): Perspectives on the Relationship between the Old and New Testaments*, edited by John S. Feinberg, 1221–761. Wheaton: Crossway, 1988. Kindle.

Feinberg, John S., ed. *Continuity and Discontinuity (Essays in Honor of S. Lewis Johnson, Jr.): Perspectives on the Relationship between the Old and New Testaments*. Wheaton: Crossway, 1988. Kindle.

Gorman, Michael J. "You Shall Be Cruciform for I am Cruciform: Paul's Trinitarian Reconstruction of Holiness." In *Holiness and Ecclesiology in the New Testament*, edited by Kent E. Brower and Andy Johnson, 148–66. Grand Rapids: Eerdmans, 2007.

Greene, Joseph R. "The Spirit in the Temple: Bridging the Gap between Old Testament Absence and New Testament Assumption." *JETS* 55.4 (2012) 717–42.

Gregerman, Adam. "Comparative Christian Hermeneutical Approaches to the Land Promises to Abraham." *Cross Currents* 64.3 (2014) 410–25.

Gundry, Robert H. *Commentary on the New Testament*. Peabody, MA: Hendrickson, 2010.

Hagner, Donald. "How "New" Is the New Testament?: Continuity and Discontinuity between the Old Testament (Formative Judaism) and the New Testament (Early Christianity)." *AJPS* 19.2 (2016) 99–107.

Hartley, J. E. "Day of Atonement." In *DOTP*, edited by T. Desmond Alexander and David W. Baker, 54–61. Downers Grove: InterVarsity, 2003.

———. "Holy and Holiness, Clean and Unclean." In *DOTP*, edited by T. Desmond Alexander and David W. Baker, 420-31. Downers Grove: InterVarsity, 2003.

Hays, Daniel J. *The Temple and the Tabernacle: A Study of God's Dwelling Places from Genesis to Revelation*. Grand Rapids, MI: Baker, 2016.

Hess, Richard S., and Elmer A. Martens, eds. *War in the Bible and Terrorism in the Twenty-First Century*. Winona Lake, IN: Eisenbrauns, 2008.

Horton, Stanley M. *Acts: A Logion Press Commentary*. Springfield, MO: Gospel Publishing House, 2001. Kindle.

Hoskins, Paul M. *Jesus as the Fulfillment of the Temple in the Gospel of John*. Paternoster Biblical Monographs. Eugene, OR: Wipf & Stock, 2006.

Houston, W. J. "Foods, Clean and Unclean." In *DOTP*, edited by T. Desmond Alexander and David W. Baker, 326-36. Downers Grove: InterVarsity, 2003.

Johnston, Philip, and Peter Walker, eds. *The Land of Promise: Biblical, Theological, and Contemporary Perspectives*. Downers Grove: InterVarsity, 2000.

Kaiser, Walter C., Jr. "Israel and its Land in Biblical Perspective." In *The Old Testament in the Life of God's People: Essays in Honor of Elmer A. Martens*, edited by Jon M. Isaak and E. A. Martens, 245-56. Winona Lake, IN: Eisenbrauns, 2009.

———. "Kingdom Promises as Spiritual and National." In *Continuity and Discontinuity (Essays in Honor of S. Lewis Johnson, Jr.): Perspectives on the Relationship between the Old and New Testaments*, edited by John S. Feinberg, 5950-6332. Wheaton: Crossway, 1988. Kindle.

———. *The Promise-Plan of God: A Biblical Theology of the Old and New Testaments*. 2nd ed. Grand Rapids: Zondervan, 2008.

Karakolis, Christos. "Church and Nation in the New Testament: The Formation of the Pauline Communities." *SVTQ* 57.3-4 (2013) 361-80.

Kattathara, Thomas S. J. *The Snag of the Sword: An Exegetical Study of Luke 22:35-38*. Frankfurt: Peter Lang GmbH, Internationaler Verlag der Wissenschaften, 2014.

Keener, Craig S. *The IVP Bible Background Commentary*. Downers Grove: InterVarsity, 1993.

———. "One New Temple in Christ (Eph. 2:11-22; Acts 21:27-29; Mark 11:17; John 4:20-24)." *AJPS* 12.1 (2009) 75-92.

———. *Romans: A New Covenant Commentary*. Cambridge: Lutterworth, 2009.

———. *The Spirit in the Gospels and Acts: Divine Purity and Power*. Grand Rapids: Baker Academic, 1997.

Kelle, Brad E., and Frank R. Ames, eds. *Writing and Reading War: Rhetoric, Gender, and Ethics in Biblical and Modern Contexts*. Atlanta: SBL, 2008.

Klooster, Fred H. "The Biblical Method of Salvation: A Case for Continuity." In *Continuity and Discontinuity (Essays in Honor of S. Lewis Johnson, Jr.): Perspectives on the Relationship between the Old and New Testaments*, edited by John S. Feinberg, 2631-3268. Wheaton: Crossway, 1988. Kindle.

Ladd, G. E. *A Theology of the New Testament*. Rev. ed. Grand Rapids: Eerdmans, 1993.

BIBLIOGRAPHY

Latourette, Kenneth Scott. *A History of Christianity, Volume 1: to A. D. 1500.* Rev. ed. San Francisco: HarperCollins, 1975.

Longenecker, Richard N. "Paul's Vision of the Church and Community Formation in His Major Missionary Letters." In *Community Formation in the Early Church and the Church Today*, edited by Richard N. Longenecker, 73–88. Peabody, MA: Hendrickson, 2002.

Marshall, I. Howard. "Congregation and Ministry in the Pastoral Epistles." In *Community Formation in the Early Church and the Church Today*, edited by Richard N. Longenecker, 105–25. Peabody, MA: Hendrickson, 2002.

Martens, Elmer A. "'O Land, Land, Land'": Reading the Earth Story in Both Testaments." In *The Old Testament in the Life of God's People: Essays in Honor of Elmer A. Martens*, edited by Jon M. Isaak and E. A. Martens, 223–44. Winona Lake, IN: Eisenbrauns, 2009.

———. "The People of God." In *Central Themes in Biblical Theology: Mapping Unity in Diversity*, edited by Scott J. Hafemann and Paul R. House, 225–53. Grand Rapids: Baker Academic, 2007.

———. "Toward Shalom: Absorbing the Violence." In *War in the Bible and Terrorism in the Twenty-First Century*, edited by Richard S. Hess and Elmer A. Martens, 33–58. Winona Lake, IN: Eisenbrauns, 2008.

Martin, Dale B. "Jesus in Jerusalem: Armed and Not Dangerous." *JSNT* 37:1 (September 2014) 3–24.

Martin, John A. "Luke." In *The Bible Knowledge Commentary: An Exposition of the Scriptures*, vol. 2, edited by J. F. Walvoord and R. B. Zuck, 260. Wheaton: Victor, 1985.

Martin, Oren R. *Bound for the Promised Land: The Land Promise in God's Redemptive Plan.* Downers Grove: InterVarsity, 2015.

Moo, Douglas J. "Romans." In *New Bible Commentary: 21st Century Edition*, edited by D. A. Carson et al., 1152–53. 4th ed. Downers Grove: InterVarsity, 1994.

Moulder, James. "Romans 13 and Conscientious Disobedience." *JTSA* 21 (1977) 13–23.

Moyise, Steve. "Dialogical Intertextuality." In *Exploring Intertextuality: Diverse Strategies for New Testament Interpretation of Texts*, edited by Steve Moyise and B. J. Oropeza, 346–708. Eugene, OR: Wipf & Stock, 2016. Kindle.

Moyise, Steve, and B. J. Oropeza, eds. *Exploring Intertextuality: Diverse Strategies for New Testament Interpretation of Texts.* Eugene, OR: Wipf & Stock, 2016. Kindle.

Noll, S. F. "Tabernacle, Temple." In *EDT*, edited by Walter A. Elwell, 1165–67. Grand Rapids: Baker, 2001.

Nunnally, Wave. *The Book of Acts.* Springfield, MO: Global University, 2007.

Oakes, Peter. "Made Holy by the Holy Spirit: Holiness and Ecclesiology in Romans." In *Holiness and Ecclesiology in the New Testament*, edited by Kent E. Brower and Andy Johnson, 167–83. Grand Rapids: Eerdmans, 2007.

Origen. *Contra Celsus (Celsum).* In *Ante-Nicene Fathers, Vol. 4*, edited by Alexander Roberts et al., translated by Frederick Crombie, book VII: 26. Buffalo: Christian Literature, 1885. http://www.newadvent.org/fathers/04167.htm

Bibliography

Oswalt, John N. "Theology of the Pentateuch." In *DOTP*, edited by T. Desmond Alexander and David W. Baker, 845–59. Downers Grove: InterVarsity, 2003.

Perrin, Nicholas. *Jesus the Temple*. Grand Rapids: Baker Academic, 2010.

Petersen, Rodney. "Continuity and Discontinuity: The Debate throughout Church History." In *Continuity and Discontinuity (Essays in Honor of S. Lewis Johnson, Jr.): Perspectives on the Relationship between the Old and New Testaments*, edited by John S. Feinberg, 226–606. Wheaton: Crossway, 1988. Kindle.

Rad, Gerhard von. "The Promised Land and Yahweh's Land in the Hexateuch." In *The Problem of the Hexateuch*, edited by Gerhard von Rad, translated by E. W. Truman Dicken, 79–93. London: Oliver & Boyd, 1966.

Rad, Gerhard von. *Holy War in Ancient Israel*. Grand Rapids: Eerdmans, 1991. Translated by Marva J. Dawn. 3rd edition of *Der Heilige Krieg im alten Israel* (Göttingen: Vandenhoeck & Ruprecht, 1958).

Robertson, O. Palmer. "A New Covenant Perspective on the Land." In *The Land of Promise: Biblical, Theological and Contemporary Perspectives*, edited by Philip Johnston and Peter Walker, 121–41. Downers Grove: InterVarsity, 2000.

Routledge, Robin. *Old Testament Theology: A Thematic Approach*. Downers Grove: InterVarsity, 2008.

Sanders, E. P. "Jerusalem and Its Temple in the Beginnings of the Christian Movement." *JQJLT* 46:2 (1997) 189–96.

Saucy, Robert L. *The Case for Progressive Dispensationalism: The Interface between Dispensational and Non-Dispensational Theology*. Grand Rapids: Zondervan, 1993.

———. "Israel and the Church: A Case for Discontinuity." In *Continuity and Discontinuity (Essays in Honor of S. Lewis Johnson, Jr.): Perspectives on the Relationship between the Old and New Testaments*, edited by John S. Feinberg, 4940–5421. Wheaton: Crossway, 1988. Kindle.

Schertz, Mary H. "Swords and Prayer." In *Struggles for Shalom: Peace and Violence across the Testaments*, edited by Laura L. Brenneman and Brad D. Schantz, 116–23. Eugene, OR: Pickwick, 2014.

Schnittjer, Gary E. *The Torah Story: An Apprenticeship on the Pentateuch*. Grand Rapids: Zondervan, 2006.

Schreiner, Thomas R. *40 Questions about Christians and Biblical Law*. 40 Questions Series. Grand Rapids: Kregel Academic & Professional, 2010.

———. "The Commands of God." In *Central Themes in Biblical Theology: Mapping Unity in Diversity*, edited by Scott J. Hafemann and Paul R. House, 66–101. Grand Rapids: Baker Academic, 2007.

Sweeney, James P. "Jesus, Paul, and the Temple: An Exploration of Some Patterns of Continuity." *JETS* 46:4 (2003) 605–31.

Thielman, Frank. *The Law and the New Testament: The Question of Continuity*. New York: Crossroads, 1999.

Thomas, Heath A. "A Neglected Witness to "Holy War" in the Writings." In *Holy War in the Bible: Christian Morality and an Old Testament Problem*, edited by Paul Copan et al., 68–86. Downers Grove: IVP Academic, 2013.

Thompson, James W. *The Church according to Paul: Rediscovering the Community Conformed to Christ*. Grand Rapids: Baker, 2014.

Townsend, Jeffrey L. "Fulfillment of the Land Promise in the Old Testament." *BSac* 142 (Oct–Dec 1985) 320–37.

Trebilco, Paul. "Early Christian Communities in the Greco-Roman City: Perspectives on Urban Ministry from the New Testament." *Ex Auditu* 29 (2013) 25–48.

VanGemeren, Willem. "Systems of Continuity." In *Continuity and Discontinuity (Essays in Honor of S. Lewis Johnson, Jr.): Perspectives on the Relationship between the Old and New Testaments*, edited by John S. Feinberg, 613–1216. Wheaton: Crossway, 1988. Kindle.

Walker, Peter. "The Land and Jesus Himself." In *The Land of Promise: Biblical, Theological and Contemporary Perspectives*, edited by Philip Johnston and Peter Walker, 100–120. Downers Grove: InterVarsity, 2000.

———. "The Land in the Apostle's Writings." In *The Land of Promise: Biblical, Theological and Contemporary Perspectives*, edited by Philip Johnston and Peter Walker, 81–99. Downers Grove: InterVarsity, 2000.

Wall, R. W. "Intertextuality, Biblical." In *DNTB*, edited by Stanley E. Porter and Craig A. Evans, 541–51. Downers Grove: IVP Academic, 2000.

Waltke, Bruce K. "Kingdom Promises as Spiritual." In *Continuity and Discontinuity (Essays in Honor of S. Lewis Johnson, Jr.): Perspectives on the Relationship between the Old and New Testaments*, edited by John S. Feinberg, 5425–949. Wheaton: Crossway, 1988. Kindle.

Waltke, Bruce K., with Charles Yu. *An Old Testament Theology: An Exegetical, Canonical, and Thematic Approach*. Grand Rapids: Zondervan, 2007.

Walton, J. Harvey and John H. Walton, *The Lost World of the Israelite Conquest: Covenant, Retribution, and the Fate of the Canaanites*. Downers Grove: IVP Academic, 2017.

Wardle, Timothy S. *Continuity and Discontinuity: The Temple and Early Christian Identity*. Dissertation. Duke University, 2008. https://www.preteristarchive.com/Books/pdf/2008_wardle_the-temple-and-early-christian-identity.pdf

Wenell, Karen J. *Jesus and Land: Sacred and Social Space in Second Temple Judaism*. New York: T. & T. Clark, 2007.

Wesley, John. *Explanatory Notes upon the New Testament, Vol. 1: Matthew to Acts*, Reprint, Grand Rapids: Baker, 1983.

Wheaton, David H. "1 Peter." In *New Bible Commentary: 21st Century Edition*, edited by D. A. Carson et al., 1376. 4th ed. Downers Grove: InterVarsity, 1994.

Williamson, Paul R. "Covenant." In *DOTP*, edited by T. Desmond Alexander and David W. Baker, 139–55. Downers Grove: InterVarsity, 2003.

———. "Promise and Fulfillment: the Territorial Inheritance." In *The Land of Promise: Biblical, Theological, and Contemporary Perspectives*, edited by Philip Johnston and Peter Walker, 15–34. Downers Grove: InterVarsity, 2000.

Wise, M. O. "Temple, Jewish." In *DNTB*, edited by Stanley E. Porter and Craig A. Evans, 1167–83. Downers Grove: IVP Academic, 2000.

Witherington III, Ben. *New Testament History: A Narrative Account*. Grand Rapids: Baker, 2001. Kindle.

Witmer, John A. "Romans." In *The Bible Knowledge Commentary: An Exposition of the Scriptures*, edited by J. F. Walvoord and R. B. Zuck, 2:453–54. Wheaton: Victor, 1985.

Woudstra, Marten H. "Israel and the Church: A Case for Continuity." In *Continuity and Discontinuity (Essays in Honor of S. Lewis Johnson, Jr.): Perspectives on the Relationship between the Old and New Testaments*, edited by John S. Feinberg, 4537–939. Wheaton: Crossway, 1988. Kindle.

Wright, Christopher J. H. *God's People in God's Land: Family, Land, and Property in the Old Testament*. Grand Rapids: Eerdmans, 1990.

Wright, N. T. *How God Became King: The Forgotten Story of the Gospels*. New York: HarperCollins, 2012.

———. *Jesus and the Victory of God*. Minneapolis: Fortress, 1996.

———. *The New Testament and the People of God*. Minneapolis: Fortress, 1992.

———. *Paul and the Faithfulness of God*. Minneapolis: Fortress, 2013. Kindle.

Yoder, John H. *The Politics of Jesus: Vicit Agnus Noster*. 2nd ed. Grand Rapids: Eerdmans, 1994.

www.ingramcontent.com/pod-product-compliance
Lightning Source LLC
Chambersburg PA
CBHW071441160426
43195CB00013B/1997